"The wind of God's Spir[ ]
His people scatter, multip[ ]
New Zealand have gone to the core of God's heart to share in practical Kiwi fashion some creative ways to obey. Their final pages alone are a treasure trove of summaries and statistics well worth the read. May God use this book to mobilize His priceless bride, the Church."

Mike Schrage
Executive Director
Good News Productions International

"*Missions Abandoned* does more than inform followers of Jesus, it challenges us to re-evaluate our commitment to missions and our passion for the lost. As you read this book you will not just be encouraged by the inspiring stories, you will want to be able to tell your own stories of living your life on mission."

Kyle Idleman
Teaching Pastor at Southeast Christian Church
Louisville, Kentucky

"Evangelism is a strange word in too many church circles. But for Andrew, it's at the center of who he is, it's the lifestyle he lives, and it's attractive and wonderfully infectious. God has called him to not only reach out to a hurting world, but to train others to embrace their own personal calls to compassionately and practically communicate the good news of the gospel of Christ. *Missions Abandoned* has been birthed out of a deep well of real world experience and will no doubt become a textbook for modern day outreach. I'm so thankful for his obedience to the Lord in getting his knowledge, experience and teachings into these pages!"

Phil Joel
Lead singer of Zealand Worship
Founder of deliberatePeople ministries

"Andrew Jit has been a personal friend and partner in ministry for many years. He is serious about the issue that should be at the forefront of every pastor's mind: discipleship. I'm encouraged that the next generation of leaders is digging deeply into the things that really matter. This book will be helpful in continuing the discipleship dialogue. And I personally appreciate the effort of Andrew and Owen to provide practical tips for those of us in the trenches on how to transform the local church into a disciple-making family of believers."

Rusty Russell
Lead Pastor, New Day Christian Church
Port Charlotte, Florida

"In this book, *Missions Abandoned*, Andrew Jit shares the same passion for global outreach that has shaped our ministry here in Savannah for the past 30 years. This is a call to build a ministry that is both spiritually deep and as wide as the world!"

Cam Huxford
Lead Pastor, Compassion Christian Church
Savannah, Georgia

"*Missions Abandoned* is an excellent resource with a fresh, practical and unique insight into how individuals and Churches view missions. Convictions that I had were reinforced, a lot of new ideas brought to light and some surprises were brought out. Anyone involved in missions on any level will benefit from what Andrew Jit and Owen Jennings have brought to light in *Missions Abandoned*. The Great Commandment and the Great Commission can be better carried out after you read this book."

Dermot O'Mahony
Senior Pastor, Elevate Community Church, Limerick, Ireland

"*Missions Abandoned* should be required reading for every new believer! With the unique candor of Kiwis, Andrew Jit and Owen Jennings extend a compelling call to discover the mission heart of God. Then with the experience of an effective mission leader in the American church, Andrew delivers a comprehensive strategy to live it out! As a church planter, this book is now one of my top recommendations for new church leaders."

Greg Marksberry
Director, Florida Church Partners
Lead Pastor, Thrive Church, Orlando, Florida

"If every leader and missions department in churches today will read this book with an open mind, their biblical vision will be opened up for missions, their ways of supporting missions will improve, their commitment for the Great Commission given by the Lord will have the right perspective in the life of the church and the direction of the church will start rising higher on the spiritual ladder. This book is an eye opener as it explains the present situation of church, the misconceptions and practices regarding missions, and then suggestions of how to get to the right path. Andrew and Owen draw attention to the church for the need to pray, to be engaged, to get involved with the mission field, both at home and abroad. They challenge the church to study and follow the Scriptures to understand that mission is not a choice, neither to put missions at the tail-end of the church budget—instead, it is a biblical mandate."

Dr. Jay Henry
Director of Bethlehem Living Water, India

"Two brothers from New Zealand have put together a book filled with encouragement and sometimes shocking challenges for the body of Christ in regard to bringing the Good News of Jesus to the ends of the earth. The stories, examples and Scripture-based teachings will not fail to inspire and energize every sincere disciple of Jesus who has the privilege of reading them. With David Platt-like directness, Andrew and Owen make things plain concerning our responsibility as disciples of Jesus to spread His teaching to all the ethne, to rescue the oppressed and to make known the presence of the Kingdom of God.

This book is also practical. Each chapter concludes with helpful ideas for application in both a personal and a church setting. Buy this book and give it to those whose hearts are passionate about knowing Jesus and making Him known to every nation! Also, buy this book and give it to those whose hearts need an awakening to the incredible privilege that we have as servants of the Most High!"

Dr. Christopher DeWelt
Director of Intercultural Studies, Ozark Christian College
Joplin, Missouri

"Our church was launched with a love for missions. Somewhere along the way, that passion became linked to a line item in a budget. For years, I have watched Andrew apply the principles you are going to read. I've watched our kids, our young adults, our working and retired adults find their place in the Great Commission. I've watched as our church rekindled a love for missions that supersedes money. I've watched a church become more like Jesus!"

Craig Grammer
Senior Minister, First Christian Church
Springfield, Ohio

"First, take a heart for missions and evangelism. Combine that with a passion to see people grow up in their faith. Then, add in a huge dash of home-grown experience in one of the most unreached countries in the world. What you'll get is the recipe for this book! I have had the privilege of working alongside Andrew Jit in the States. And even as a young man, his heart beat fast for missions. And now, years later, he has put together an important work with plenty of convicting reminders to refocus church leaders on the Great Commission. I was inspired by the personal stories and challenged by the bold and direct approach. I highly recommend that you read this book and then say anew, 'Here am I Lord! Send me!'"

Brian Jobe
Senior Pastor at Chandler Christian Church
Chandler, Arizona

"This book, *Missions Abandoned*, is so needed and very well done. It is a book of Bible exposition and a practical mission-strategy. This book brings a fresh perspective to the greatest mission of all. Andrew and Owen's insights have re-energized me to go into my ministry field and involve in God's Mission tirelessly. It has enhanced my understanding of partnership in Christian holistic mission. The helpful tips and insights that Andrew and Owen provide in this remarkable book will help you to effectively carry out your biblical responsibility in your mission field. You too can experience the joy of leading someone to Christ. I trust that you will catch a great excitement through this book as you read how God is at work in our neighborhoods, in our business and at countless venues around the globe."

Niranjan Adhikary
Director of Ray of Hope Nepal

"If you have a small flame burning in your soul and you have a gnawing sense that you and your church could have much more global impact for Christ, then *Missions Abandoned* could put wood on your fire. Andrew and Owen deliver part devotional, part conversation, part story, part missions handbook as they share their burden for helping Christians and churches walk in tune with Christ in reaching the world. It's not a book to skim—it's one to soak in, as you let your mind and heart marinate in the frequently cited Scriptures on God's plan for His people and the world.

Dick Alexander
International Consultant, CMF International

"Nicely packed with both the information and the tools for transformation in amplifying missional living, *Missions Abandoned* is approachable reading that the authors have made incredibly simple to begin applying. On both individual and small group levels, the content is consistently given "handles" for real life experimentation and implementation. And the authors are practitioners too; no ivory tower here! The result: readable, digestible, implementable tools to arm ourselves and our churches for deeper and more fulfilling engagement in Christ's mission. Get it, read it, live it and watch in eager anticipation of what the Lord will do."

Brian Gibson
Executive Director, TRAIN International

MISSIONS

ABANDONED

RE-ESTABLISHING MISSIONS AS A PRIORITY IN OUR LIVES AND CHURCHES

ANDREW JIT &
OWEN JENNINGS

To my Pa,

*A man who taught me what it means
to truly follow Jesus and be His disciple.*

To my Jamie,

My lovely bride that I love doing life with.

ANDREW

To Doreen,

who best personifies the love, graciousness and patience of Jesus.

OWEN

Note: Andrew is Owen's nephew. Owen married Andrew and Jamie and plays an important role in their lives. The book is a product of their closeness, respect for each other and the influence of people like Jim Jennings, Andrew's Pa and Owen's father.

Contents

Foreword

If I were to say that we are in the midst of a cultural "sea change" among churches in the USA, perhaps the most common reaction might be, "Duh." Remember Sunday night services? Remember pipe organs? How long since you sang from a 'hymnbook?' And tell me again about 'Sunday School...' or even 'youth group,' for that matter. And what about the 'Missions Committee,' 'faith promise,' and the annual 'missions Sunday?' In fact, when did you last hear a missionary speak in your church on Sunday morning?

In the midst of all this change, there are still some courageous innovators who figure out how to be relevant. They discern the times, contextualize their message (like any good missionary), and make it work. Andrew Jit is one of those characters.

In this book, *Missions Abandoned: Re-establishing missions as a priority in our lives and churches*, Andrew Jit and his co-author, Owen Jennings, describe reality as they see it—and then they help us deal with it. They help you define missions, both practically and biblically, then review a clear theology of missions, thus giving us the Bible basis and our 'reason for being.' They make a strong case for integrating missions not as a committee function, thereby delegating it to a few people in one Sunday School class, but rather as the central core work of the entire church and its individual members. Departing from the status quo, they propose a bold new vision that could help any outreach pastor, as well as any missions committee, frame up the future. They aren't afraid to deal with 'sacred cows.' In fact, they tackle them head-on. They offer a rich set of case studies, along with lots of examples and resources. In painting a picture of the future, they are both idealistic and practical, all at the same time.

I've known Andrew for many years. His background growing up in New Zealand does more than give him a cross-cultural look and feel. (His accent does seem to work in his favor, by the way). The truth is, bringing his Pacific Rim origins to the heartlands of the USA provides him with just the kind of broad cultural context that helps him appreciate the past while valuing the present. And when he speaks of the other side of the world, well—he gets it. He grew up there. Plus—his years in youth ministry give him valuable insights on students of all ages. But just as importantly, his zeal for the Word gives him an unquenchable fire for the Cause. He BELIEVES in what he teaches. He CARES about the lost—as well as those he's seeking to influence. And most importantly, he MODELS what he thinks. In other words, he's authentic.

Sitting in behind Andrew and his still youthful drive and energy is the lifetime of experience and wisdom of Owen Jennings. It is a powerful combination that gives Missions Abandoned such width in subject matter and depth in quality material. Owen has not just been a senior leader in several areas of business and politics in New Zealand but he has been heavily involved in outreach locally and internationally having set up and audited partnerships in many third world countries. He has also made a major contribution to the work of Bright Hope World which is such a key part of this book. Readers are tapping into a rich vein of authenticity and hands on participation.

I'll never forget the first time Andrew invited me to stop by and visit his 'MiT' class. (I wondered if they would all be math and computer whizzes). I soon learned that he wasn't using 'MiT' to describe a college in Boston. Rather, he was full-on focused on 'Missionaries in Training.' Either way it was working.

Before I knew what was happening, six young people had shown up, as they do every week, for training, mentoring, and inspiration. Andrew is on a roll. Not long afterward, he asked if he could bring a few students to Emerald Hills (Team Expansion's international training and sending base) in Louisville, KY. The students who came were so seriously on task that we treated them all as though they were college level, even though he had incorporated several high school students. Later, on another visit to MiT, his group of trainees had grown to ten, some of whom were ready to head off to some of the most restrictive nations on earth. Several took part in a Team Expansion short-term trip this past summer—and finished in a magnificent fashion. We even overlooked the fact that a couple of them were high-schoolers (our trips are normally for college and older). We're glad we did. They outperformed many college students in their preparation and level of maturity.

Frankly, I'm not sure how Andrew keeps finding so many new willing workers at his church in Springfield, Ohio. The strange thing is, he's also attracting others from OUTSIDE his church. It's like he DRAWS them... like a magnet. They seek him out, perhaps because he cares for them so much ... or maybe it IS his New Zealand accent, I don't know. (I'm kidding.) Either way, he's on to something. And whatever it is, we have to replicate it.

So many of us told Andrew he should write down what he does. Once again, his 'Midas-like touch' has turned to gold. In the pages that follow, please don't skip over all the sidebars and boxes. They're filled with examples... real people Andrew and Owen have met or heard about in their travels somewhere. That's what you get when you work with guys like Andrew and Owen: real people... real stories... real life. So these pages are not filled with things they have observed others do... or stories from books others have written. These pages are vintage Andrew and Owen. And all of us should read, listen and apply. Then rinse and repeat. Their work is as challenging as it is productive. They do not sell out quality for quantity. Ask any of Andrew's MiT'ers and they'll tell you the same: He cares. He walks alongside them. I wasn't surprised a couple of months ago when he asked if he could just 'pop in' on a couple of his workers serving on a short-term trip with our organization. To put things in perspective, he wanted to 'pop in' on them while they were serving in northern Ghana. When I told him the trip there would likely take three days from Ohio, he didn't even blink. That's what Andrew does.

So when you read Missions Abandoned, please—on behalf of unreached people everywhere—watch, listen, learn and act. Because you're seeing masters at work. May God bless the time they have invested here. May it not be wasted on us as we seek to reproduce it.

Doug Lucas
President, Team Expansion

Introduction

This is a book about you, your church, and missions.

One of the amazing aspects of being a Christian is that our awesome, all-powerful God has made each of us His partner in the greatest vocation of all time—building His church by winning the world. Yes, that is the way He has set up His most critical mission of saving people from eternal destruction—a partnership—Jesus and me, Jesus and you, working in a tight team to bring salvation to a lost world. What a privilege. What a team to be selected for.

Imagine a scene. You are standing watching a frightening spectacle. Out in the harbor, a boat is rapidly sinking. A whole bunch of people are on board. They have no life jackets, they cannot swim, and their situation is absolutely without hope. You see family members, your brother and a sister on board, then a neighbor and a workmate. Oh, the despair.

You get a tap on the shoulder. It's Jesus. "I want you to help Me save those people." "Nah, I can't do it." "Look, I am Jesus. I am God's Son. I will be with you all the way. You can access all My resources. When we get there, I will resuscitate them, carry them to shore, and see that they are all okay. We can work together."

"No, not me. Get someone else."

It is our belief that missions, discipling, evangelizing, and caring for the underprivileged, the needy, and those suffering from injustice, have slipped way too far down personal and church priority lists. Many Christians have abandoned the clear commands we are meant to follow. We are spiritually poorer for not responding to what Jesus requires us to do.

Every minute of the day, hundreds die around the world without a knowledge of Christ as their Savior. They haven't been taught the great truths of the Bible. Others suffer gross injustices. Many live in abject poverty and misery, yet, as believers, we hold answers. Answers that work.

In the remainder of this book, we propose that discipling involves a holistic, life-long commitment to evangelizing, growing the faith of others, and dealing with poverty and injustice. This is what Jesus taught. God has chosen to rely on us as believers, empowered by His Holy Spirit. He could choose a myriad of ways to bring sinners to repentance; after all He is Almighty God capable of anything. However, His plan included us as His primary means of the unsaved hearing about and responding to the message of Calvary's love and forgiveness. We are letting Him down. We have abandoned the mission.

> **The Purpose of Missions Abandoned**
>
> 1. Missions has become a low priority for Christians and their churches – we want to help change that.
>
> 2. The cornerstones we promote are obedience and passion – **obedience** to the command of Christ and **passion** for the lost.
>
> 3. We need to be connected to Jesus to be effective for Jesus.

Our message is simple, but very direct. Even blunt. We all need to re-commit to Christ's command and His priority. Christ does not give us an option. The Great Commission isn't just a great suggestion or an optional ministry: it is the ministry of our lives. Our churches need to sharpen their focus on evangelizing and discipling. We believe that if you are a disciple, then missions is your DNA. Jesus has called us daily to live on a mission with Him.

The biblical authority on which we make claims throughout this book comes from Matthew's gospel: "Go and make disciples of all nations ... teaching them to obey…" (Matthew 28:19).

The book is a little bit of theology and a heap of practical stuff. We examine the theology because God's Word is sharper than a two-edged sword and can do much more to convince and convict you about missions than we can. It is the 'why' part. The practical bit or the 'how' is centered around some simple ideas to improve your discipling. We refer to a missionary ministry called Bright Hope World because we have been involved in their work and have seen how God has blessed their approach to Matthew 28:19.

This is not a novel, nor is it a complete study book. It is more a collection of ideas, stories, robust challenges, suggestions and encouragements based on our experiences. Serving God in missions can be challenging—even dangerous at times—but it is immensely satisfying.

In spite of the criticisms and warnings, we are hugely optimistic about the potential and future of missions. Our interaction with young people shows a new generation that has buckets of confidence, is unfazed by past hang-ups, and just wants to get out and do things.

They do need a stronger doctrinal base from which to launch, and they need practical input on the "how." Should we harness this wave of millennials, gently steer them into the truths of God's Word, display some sensitive leadership from pastors and elders, and offer practical, proven, workable solutions—the world could then be our oyster. In this regard, we have a section later in the book on a brand new ministry started by Andrew called MiT. MiT stands for Missionaries in Training and is a ministry designed to help young people live on mission daily with Jesus. It is a strategy for global missions multiplication through intentional, relational, and deliberate discipleship for fueling young people's passions for a global purpose. Check it out. It has much to offer our young people.

Too many churches are unbalanced in their activity—too much focus on worship only, and not worship leading to missions out of an overflowing heart. An underperformance in missions does not arise from not knowing what to do—it is mostly an unwillingness to do what we already know. It is a paucity of passion and obedience, not a paucity of understanding. We serve most effectively out of appreciation of our magnificent, merciful God.

We hope you will be challenged to actually do something specific and meaningful as you read through these stories. We are praying fervently that you will be inspired by the work that is happening, arrested by the Spirit, transformed by the words of Christ, and motivated to start a new phase of mission activity in your life, the life of your family, and the life of your church. The church needs a sea change, a cultural tsunami of change refocusing on God's command, and it starts with you, now. You will not be disappointed. 2 Kings 7:9 says, "Then they said to each other, 'We're not doing right. This is the day of good news and we are keeping it to ourselves…. Let's go at once.'"

William Carey, missionary and Bible translator who is known as the 'father of modern missions' said, "Is not the commission of our Lord still binding upon us? Can we not do more than now we are doing?" While this is a book about missions, discipling, evangelizing and reaching the underprivileged, it is actually a book about the Lord our God and our personal relationship with Him. Doing what He commanded us to do is best done from a heart overflowing with a growing knowledge of and love for Him, along with a passion for the souls for which He died.

Andrew and Owen

PREFACE

Both of us, Andrew and Owen, are Kiwis—in other words, New Zealanders, although Andrew now lives in Ohio, USA and is married to a beautiful lady, Jamie. The Kiwi is our national icon, but strangely, it is a shy, half blind, nocturnal bird that cannot fly. As you would expect, some make fun of us over this.

However, the same Kiwi is exceptionally shrewd. It has adapted to its environment, learns and moves very quickly, and avoids its predators quite skillfully. Given its limitations, it achieves a great deal. It 'punches away above its weight.' For a small country of four million, we produced Lydia Ko, the world's best female golfer; Peter Jackson, who made the Lord of the Rings and the Hobbit movies; Sir Edmund Hillary, the first man to climb Mount Everest; Lorde, the celebrity singer; Steve Adams, the Thunder's man; Scott Dixon, four-time IndyCar Champion; Ernest Rutherford, who first split the atom; and the world's best rugby players, the All Blacks. When you are small and on the bottom of the world, you have to fight for recognition and status. That is why we want to share the story of Bright Hope World, a revelation in successful missions work—largely unknown, but a story that needs exposure.

Kiwis are well known for their blunt and straight talk. We are not big on delicate niceties. We are blunt in this book, too, because Jesus is blunt in His commands to be His followers. If you want to throw some stones at us over what we have written, help yourself. You will be surprised how hard it is to find us!

Seriously though, we suggest you visit Andrew or jump on a plane and come down to New Zealand and join us for a La Mai coffee, where we can talk through the good and the bad in this book. We are still learning and would appreciate your input. The bonus is that you would see one of the most beautiful countries in the world. We may be small and far away, but we can package some magnificent scenery into a very small space.

Friends, we can't choose to obey some commands of Jesus and ignore the others. The command to preach the good news was given to each and every one of us to do. We can't leave it for someone else to do. To fully grasp this task, known as the Great Commission, we must first understand God's mission. Missions exist because God exists. We must understand that our mission is rooted in God's mission. It is easy to lose the grandeur of God's mission: Man should glorify God by knowing Him, worshipping Him and making Him known throughout the world.

We are praying for you as you read this book. We pray it will challenge and convict you, and give you practical ideas for pursuing missions in your own life.

Chapter 1

Reacquaint

Getting to know missions again. What constitutes missions and discipling that Christ commands us to do?

"Expect great things from God. Attempt great things for God."
— William Carey

"It is the duty of every Christian to be Christ to his neighbor."
— Martin Luther

Jesus knelt to pray. He was facing the most momentous event in all history. The Righteous Father was about to mete out on Him the most awful punishment. So what does this Jesus do? Cry for help for Himself? No. He prays for His twelve brave, but vulnerable, followers. In a display of sacrifice, love and selflessness, He asks His Father to protect them, unify them, overflow their joy and sanctify them. Jesus reminded His Father He was leaving them in the world for a mission. Rather than take them straight to glory, He had a task for them. The mission was that through them and those who follow, every man and woman everywhere, might know the saving power of Jesus and grow in their faith and knowledge of Him.

As you start reading this book, we are praying for you—praying that you will become reacquainted with what the Bible says about missions and acquainted with the opportunity. We are asking for you what Jesus asked for Peter, Andrew, James, and the other disciples that you may be infused with desire to serve Christ and obey His command to make Him known. For just as Christ was leaving the gigantic task to these rough, tough, but humbled men, so today He leaves the task to us. By His own choice, we are all He has. It is on your shoulders, my shoulders, to fulfill the most obvious and unmistakable of calls.

Our dream is for every follower of Jesus—every man, woman, child, every generation and every church—to live on mission for God. This does not necessarily mean becoming a missionary to Africa or India (although that may be the calling God has for you), but that you begin with obedience and trust and accept what is as plain as the nose on your face—you are commanded by Christ to be involved.

We believe that the normal way to think about global missions is that missions = discipleship. A lot of people believe that global missions is only about evangelism, but to be effective evangelists, we are to be devoted disciples first. A fully devoted disciple will naturally be an evangelist from the overflow of their hearts and souls as they are grounded in the Word and attuned to the Sprit of God. If you are a disciple, then missions is your DNA and you will live daily on mission with Jesus. It is who you are and how you choose to live: living radically, passionately, sacrificially for a God who wants all to be saved.

We want you to live a passionate, missional life for the Kingdom of God. Jesus has called every follower of His to be His messenger. Every disciple needs to rise up and carry the message of God's love, grace, forgiveness and redemption with them through everyday stuff of life to the world out there. This is not just our dream; this is Jesus' message to you, His disciples.

"Therefore go and make disciples of all nations, baptizing them in the name of the Father and of the Son and of the Holy Spirit, and teaching them to obey everything I have commanded you. And surely I am with you always, to the very end of the age." – Matthew 28:19-20

Jesus spent three years training these men whom He called to follow Him, shaping their lives, infusing them with enthusiasm and passion for His cause. Now He commissions them. The whole purpose of His calling disciples comes to this dramatic moment of consecration. Now, nothing else matters.

For Jesus, it's now or never. It's the big climax. His mission either takes off and the world will change forever, or His trust in twelve very ordinary guys and three years of intensive preparation will go down the creek.

It was a big call. It was a high-risk strategy. The biggest game in town was about to play out. With the indwelling power of the Holy Spirit and the enthusiasm arising from their experiencing the

Pick Me

The big game in New Zealand is rugby. We are crazier about rugby than Americans are about basketball, football or baseball.

As kids we used to make up a couple of casual teams to play in school breaks. To get a team it consisted of the two best players making alternative choices from among the rest of us. We would call out "pick me", "pick me" to try and get in the best team.

Jesus wants you in His team.

Are you calling, "Pick me?"

resurrection, the eleven and their new friends took on the world. They succeeded. We stand on their shoulders and now we have the baton.

Jesus has given the opportunity to every man and woman, young and old, regardless of position, social status, rich or poor, to join Him on this great mission. God will get His mission done, but through His amazing grace He has given us the opportunity to be used by Him for His glory. Is there any greater purpose that should bring us more joy? God specializes in using the ordinary to do amazing things, so don't think for one minute you are not qualified or this is for someone else. Jesus will use anyone who is open and willing. He can overcome our shortcomings, but He can't overcome our unavailability. Jesus sees potential in you and wants to use you.

You need to ask yourself if you are open to being used by Jesus. Do you have any interest in getting reacquainted with His commands? How many blessings do we miss out on because we are too busy? If you love Jesus, you are to be His disciple and His disciple-maker. Jesus has been calling His disciples for centuries to mission. It is our time as disciples to follow Him, to do what disciples of Jesus do: make disciples who make disciples. It is a mission that never stops. It's not a once-only occurrence. Discipling carries on, growing the individual spiritually, socially, and vocationally, investing your life in theirs so they can reproduce in the next generation. Making disciples is lifelong, and means committing to helping and improving every aspect of their lives.

If you love Jesus and want to follow Him as a disciple maker, you will want to be in a church that makes missions a very high priority. For too many churches today, missions and outreach have slipped off the radar. Churches have become worship centers, places to gather to praise and honor the Lord, but little else. Worship should be the cornerstone of a church's activity, but it should lead to more than just honoring the Lord in a worship service and being a member of a small group. Worship without missions is plain self-centeredness. It is following Jesus on our terms, not His. A Bible-based church should be able to say, "Our mission is to passionately love God and to purposefully love others including those who are lost wherever they are." They should be heavily focused on outreach locally, nationally and internationally. They ought to be deliberate and strategic.

The opportunities for mission and disciple-making have never been greater. In western countries, the percentage of Christians, especially among young people, is falling quite dramatically. Church attendance is dropping away. Surveys show greater numbers see Christians as hypocrites and irrelevant.[1] In the developing world, injustices increase. Less than half of the world's 6,900 languages have the Bible available in their tongue. The need is great. The task stands incomplete. However, the future could be exciting.

The Command to "GO"

The Greek word that Jesus used for sending out His disciples is a very strong military term. It is deliberately used by Jesus to denote authority, seriousness, urgency and compulsion. In our politically correct world we would be offended to get such a "in your face" command to follow someone and obey them. Jesus had that authority but it was balanced by His obvious love and grace.

Paul used the same word for discipling Timothy. This is why we need to sit up and listen. The great Commander in Chief has ordered us into service.

One of the very unique and special things about the Christian faith is that, contrary to all other religions, it is an act of grace and faith that provides for our entry into its benefits. I cannot work my way into righteousness no matter how hard I try or how big a sacrifice I make. I cannot puzzle my way by sheer academic reasoning and rationalizing no matter how much of an intellectual giant I may be. "For it is by grace you have been saved, through faith - and this is not from yourselves, it is the gift of God" (Ephesians 2:8).

Romans 3:22 says, "This righteousness is given through faith in Christ Jesus to those who believe." In verse 28, we are reminded that a man is "justified by faith." Where does the faith come from? "Faith comes by hearing," according to James. That is why our witness and missions work is critical in God's plan. We have to tell out something for sinners to hear. "How then, can they call on the One they have not believed in? And how can they believe in the One of whom they have not heard? And how can they hear without someone preaching to them?" (Romans 10:14)

Paul, the apostle who was very learned and quite a brilliant thinker and orator, said his fine-sounding words were useless unless there was a "demonstration of the Spirit's power so that your faith does not rest on men's wisdom but on God's power" (1 Corinthians 2:4-5). So God does the saving and faith is the key ingredient, but we are needed as preachers for all to hear.

Essential Elements of Missions

The Bible teaches that missions and discipling involves a variety of activities, including:

1.   **Discipling.** "Grow in grace and in the knowledge of our Lord and Savior, Jesus Christ" (2 Peter 3:18). "Instead speaking the truth in love, we will grow to become in every aspect the mature body of Him who is the Head, that is Christ" (Ephesians 4:15).

2.   **Evangelism.** "The Lord is not slow in keeping His promise, as some understand slowness. Instead He is patient with you, not wanting anyone to perish, but everyone to come to repentance" (2 Peter 3:9). "Always be doing the work of an evangelist" (2 Timothy 4:5). See also Acts 13:47.

3.   **Maturity.** "Work so that you may be mature" (James 1:4). "Therefore let us move beyond the elementary teachings about Christ and be taken forward to maturity" (Hebrews 6:1).

4.   **Tackling poverty.** "Speak up for those who cannot speak for themselves, for the rights of all who are destitute. Speak up and judge fairly; defend the rights of the poor and needy" (Proverbs 31:8-9).

5.   **Tackling oppression.** "Whoever oppresses the poor shows contempt for their maker but whoever is kind to the needy honors the Lord" (Proverbs 14:31).

These are the essential elements of missions and what God has called us to do. We are to follow these both locally and globally. They are laid out neatly for us in Luke chapter 4, when Jesus was launching His ministry. He was introducing Himself as the Servant of the Father, sent into the world with a mission. He claimed He was authorized to bring into reality God's longstanding plan for His people. His angle was, this is My work and now I am going to make it your work. When we do this, we will experience joy—complete joy. (Read John 15:9-17).

God is calling us—or more correctly—He is demanding that we get reacquainted with His mission for us. He has the authority as the Son of God and the One who purchased us with His own blood to command us to join the ranks of His army. He orders us, equips us, sets out the battle plan, and assures us that the main enemy is already defeated. The only gremlins left to destroy are our inner voices of fear, embarrassment and a love for going AWOL.

Let us tackle His Word with renewed vigor and determination so we can see why He has left us here and what He has in mind for us to do. Don't wait for your church to get missions back on its agenda, do your own research and study regarding what the Bible says and ask the Holy Spirit to open your eyes and heart to what God wants you to do and how He wants you to do it. Then take your passion, vision, and understanding of missions and work to help excite and ignite your church to its potential.

Relationships

It is easy to think that Jesus was wandering along the lakeside, saw some potential candidates and called them up to serve Him. They dropped everything and went into full-time work. If only it was that easy and if only it were true!

Matthew chapter 4 makes it sound like it was almost a chance encounter. However, putting the four gospel writers together (as we always should when establishing background and a complete understanding of God's Word) shows a much more powerful and planned strategy. These were men who had sat under John the Baptist's ministry. Their minds were prepared. It is not inconceivable when carefully assessing the timing, that Jesus spent up to a year working with the fishermen, talking late into the night, answering questions, eating together, discussing the weather and the local sailing derby, criticizing the government and rising taxes.

Eventually, on the back of a trust relationship, Jesus brought the conversation around to whether they would make a commitment. They had not only listened to Jesus words but they had observed His behavior. They had seen a difference. His life spoke volumes. He quietly and deliberately did things differently. He was immersed in their lives and the lives of the villagers, but every one of them could see He wasn't one of them. He stood out, not in an aggressive, contrarian manner, not in an offensive, provocative way, but they had seen His inner strength and determination, His uncompromising approach to the truth and the counter cultural actions. What they did see was love, grace and sacrifice in action. They saw a Man of prayer and power.

Say, friend, what are your relationships like?

Do those around you see you as different, but not threatening? Standing apart from the sleaze, but still engaged in everything? Discerning, but not disturbing? Jesus put it in a nutshell: "in the world but not part of the world" (John 17:13-18).

Most of us just meld into the crowd. No one sees us as different. Just another fan going to the big game of life. Struggling with work and lack of income like everyone else in the street. Challenges with kids like every mom at the school. Church? Oh yes, we go to church, but even that becomes a non-event because we tend to downplay it. As Dr. Joe Aldrich in his excellent book, *Lifestyle Evangelism*,[2] says, we are immersionists who fail to stand out in any way at any time, or we are 'rabbit hole' Christians who only come out of our burrow occasionally, look around to see we won't be caught, dash out for our Sunday fill, then scuttle back down our secure little home burrow.

With God and missions, there is no Plan B. We are it. If we fail, the weight of the lost is carried on our shoulders. If whole language groups do not even have a gospel in their own language, only the church is to blame. If injustices remain unchallenged, Christians carry a disproportionate amount of the responsibility, because Christ focused on the victims of injustice as those needing help. If poverty persists at home or in any corner of the globe, we should be the first to ask "why?" and be leading the assault against it. It is apparent that these challenges are not being conquered. It is obvious that the Christian community is not as committed as it might be.[3]

Missions is About More Than Money

A sending church visited one of their long-term missionary partners in the field for the first time with their new missions pastor. The missions pastor was stepping into a church that had a history of missions in their DNA. He was curious to see how the church was effective in their missions ministry. When asked, "How are we doing as a supporting church?" the missionary couple looked at each other nervously. Hesitantly, the husband said, "You are a great ATM machine, but not a great partner," and gave the church about a D minus. Ouch! Why was their grade so low? There was no strategy, no plan, no accountability, no encouragement and no partnership. But there was money sent out regularly. Missionaries do not need their sending church to be simply an ATM machine: they need partners who make genuine sacrifices for them.

To be involved in missions is more than just sending money. It involves us being fully committed to those with whom we partner. It takes time and investment to learn, respect and understand each other fully. It is important to listen. Jesus did. He heard the cries of the hearts of those He encountered. He was personal, intentional, flexible, and focused on the individual. People in the field need to be treated the same. Partnership means an intentional investment into their lives. They are not just some distant missionary a church may support, a partner whose name and village is hard to pronounce, or a group of people that we should occasionally pray for. We must pray intelligently and specifically for them daily, care for them genuinely through regular encouragement and support, and go spend time in their world.

The Why Factor

One of the most common questions asked when visiting an underprivileged part of the world is the "why" question:

"Why I am blessed while they are not?"

"Why was I born with _____ and they weren't?"

"Why was I born in a first world country when they have nothing?"

What we fail to grasp is that they believe they are blessed - we are just spoiled with luxuries. They oftentimes have their needs met by God, while we fail to recognize what we have around us.

Cambodia: First Mission Trip

As I (Andrew) drove over the rickety wooden bridge, the water grabbed my attention. It was sort of a highlighter green and yellow blend of sewerage and rubbish. The stench was something that stuck in my nostrils - more fumes than odor. On both banks I could see rough shacks with parts of roofs missing, no doors, and some that would be the size of your bathroom. On the water's edge, ladies did their washing, kids splashed about; men had fishing rods, hoping to catch something, anything. I stopped. This was it: I had made it to the poorest part of the city. It was a place I didn't want to be, let alone stop. It was scorching hot outside. It was an uncomfortable place, a distressing place, a place without hope.

I reluctantly got out and immediately something caught my eye. A little boy and his mates playing soccer, the beautiful game, and they were smiling from ear to ear. They had a great treasure - they had a soccer ball. This ball wasn't the typical one that you would give to your child for a birthday. No, this was a custom ball made of twine, leaves, sticks and a plastic bag to wrap it all out. No doubt they would have found these supplies floating down the river. I stood and watched in the midst of utter poverty - they were the happiest lads around. What a dichotomy: we are in the poorest part of the city, and here we see them with such joy. They motioned for me to come and play. It was hard not to. The joy of those kids was infectious. When they had enough, the mates went home and I got chatting to the boy's family. They proudly pointed out their dwelling, which wasn't much to look at, but for them, it was their castle. They asked why I was there and then asked a question that is still stuck in my mind: "Will you help the poor people of our city?"

I was thinking to myself, "Aren't you the poor people? You have a house about the size of an average bathroom, with five people sleeping here on sacks, no beds. I can see the sewerage that is seeping into your front door, the plastic wrap acting as a roof that won't survive another storm, and you have a cesspool for a river in your backyard." Yet they were content with what they had.

We have this saying in our house, "First world problems." They include problems like:

"My iPhone's battery runs out before the end of the day" – That's a real issue.

"My steak was a little overcooked, so I need a new one" – Crisis averted.

"They only had the generic store brand" – That's not cool.

"Our dishwasher is too noisy" – Hard to live with.

"We only have three choices of dressing for the salad" – Such a sacrifice.

It gets real easy to forget the true blessings in our lives. We are never content or satisfied with what we have, as the grass on the other side always looks greener. Really, what about your patch of grass? Many would love to enjoy the basics of life that we enjoy, but mostly we just overlook them.

Those who have little are typically grateful for what they do have. In some of the poorest of the poor areas, you find the most content people. As crazy as it seems to us who live under the illusion that more and more will bring more happiness, those who have little have the most joy.

Gross Injustices

Life is not fair for most of the world's population. For some, it's monstrously hideous. Injustice and exploitation is common and growing. The stories are gross and repulsive, yet we say we have the power of the living Christ - the power to break down strongholds. We say we are more than conquerors. Yes, we can easily join the fight against gross human depravity.

An Ugly, Unjust World

Oudom loved school. He had finished another day and was playing with the other boys on the clear area by the main road. He lived near a city in Cambodia. Oudom was a good-looking kid with smooth, flawless skin. He was the apple of his mother's eye. Suddenly there was a lot of shouting and what seemed to be a fight along the street. The game stopped and everyone tried to see what was happening. Oudom moved out onto the road to get a better look. Suddenly, strong arms grabbed him, and before he realized what was going on, he was bundled into a van and was being driven off at high speed.

Gagged and tied, he had no idea where he was or how long he had been in the van. All he knew was there were two other boys with him and he was very scared. After what seemed like forever, he was dragged into a house, untied and placed in front of a rather frightening looking man. The man stared at him. Without warning, he lashed out and hit Oudom in the stomach. The desperately scared, hurt boy cried out, begging to be taken home. "You live here now, you are my boy and you will do as you are told. You break the rules and you will get another whack like that."

The next day, Oudom was given food, made to shower and was given new clothes to wear. Maybe he was going home, he thought. He was shifted into a bedroom where he waited. The door opened and a large, overweight, European-looking man came into the room. He had a sickly smile on his face. "Mmm. What a pretty little man you are," he muttered. "Just do what uncle wants." He patted Oudom's shoulder, then let his hands run down his sides and front. Oudom recoiled in horror. "Just take me home," he cried. Instead, the man began ripping his clothes and pushed him onto the bed. Suddenly the most unbelievable pain tore through his little body and he blacked out.

No excuses for such a dramatic story. That is happening daily. If we abhor such filthy perversion, how much more does a holy God? Yet, He has left us in charge of challenging those involved, of fighting injustice and taking a message of hope to the oppressed. Maybe we have it too good to even consider helping.

It gets real easy to forget the true blessings in our lives. We are never content or satisfied with what we have, as the grass on the other side always looks greener. Really, what about your patch of grass? Many would love to enjoy the basics of life that we enjoy, but mostly we just overlook them. Those who have little are typically grateful for what they do have. In some of the poorest of the poor areas, you find the most contented people. As crazy as it seems to us who live under the illusion that more and more will bring more happiness, those who have little have the most joy.

Missions needs to be more than just helping people for a short span. More than helping when we get emotionally wound up. It needs to be about a strategy and a plan to help people for a lifetime, for long-term sustainability. It is about giving people hope and improving their lot through giving a little that can change a lot. It is not about short-term relief or assistance to get them through a day. It is educating them for their future. It is about tackling heinous evil, hitting poverty, having a long-term partnership with a recovery plan, and sharing the love and compassion of Jesus.

The old proverb, "give a man a fish and you feed him for a day, teach him how to fish and you will feed him for a lifetime," is so true, but it is forgotten so often in the third world. Giving money and goods in these areas can become toxic charity, where it is more about the donor and their needs than about the people receiving the support. Relief is not a short-term issue -it requires long-term planning and execution. It requires dedication and an understanding of what works in the third world. Too much effort has no lasting benefit, and in many instances, leaves the recipients worse off. Humanitarian work must be accompanied with sustainable, long-term goals. It respects the poor and downtrodden and focuses solely on their needs.

The Four Mission Fields

Throughout this book, we will range over the four mission fields we are commanded by God to work in. Each of these fields need reintegrating into both our individual and church lives. The Bible indicates that missions starts with family and moves out to all

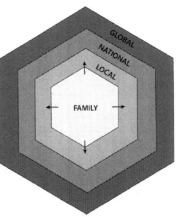

corners of the earth (John 1:41, Acts 1:8). "Declare His glory among the nations, His marvelous deeds among the peoples" (1 Chronicles 16:24).

Field 1 - Family

Our first responsibility is to our family. This is particularly so of our own children, who we need to raise in a knowledge of the Savior. God has instructed parents to be deliberate and persistent in teaching their children about salvation, faith and character.

Moses wrote, "Hear, O Israel: The Lord our God, the Lord is one. Love the Lord your God with all your heart and with all your soul and with all your strength. These commandments that I give you today are to be on your hearts. Impress them on your children. Talk about them when you sit at home and when you walk along the road, when you lie down and when you get up. Tie them as symbols on your hands and bind them on your foreheads. Write them on the doorframes of your houses and on your gates" (Deuteronomy 6:4-9).

Moses tells us that loving God should be our priority. If we are genuine in our love for the Lord as parents, and there is no inkling of hypocrisy, then that is the first step in winning our children for the Lord. Kids hate hypocrisy. When God is in the right place in our lives as parents, things go better. Our marriages are healthier. Our families are stronger. Our faith continues to grow and thrive.

Moses told parents to "impress them (the commands) on your children." The word 'impress' means to brand for life. A farmer will brand their cattle so they know which ones belong to them. God has instructed parents to impress on their children how to love God deeply and completely. From the beginning of the day to its end, we are to share God's love, grace and forgiveness. Parents are to impress on their children how to know the ways of God.

Moses teaches us that there are four key times all families can leverage time to build the faith of their children: when you sit at home, when you walk along the road, when you lie down and when you get up (Deuteronomy 6:7). It is about creating a daily rhythm of family life centered on a Jesus culture in your home. We have to be intentional in telling children about the ongoing love story between God's people and Himself. We know our role as parents is to show our children God's love through our relationship to and with them. Devoting quality time to our children both collectively and individually is critical.

In an age of snacking, eating out, skipping meals and busy households, the practice of families eating meals together is, sadly, disappearing. Where you can, reinstitute this experience and spend time during the meal to listen. Make it a rule that no electronic devices are running during this time. Take time to spend a little quality time with each child. That's a big ask, given the way we run our lives, but our children are our responsibility - we brought them into the world and we need to make the sacrifices necessary to take an interest in what they are doing. Learn to affirm the good and be strong in identifying the not so good. If you are older, you may remember the saying, "an ounce of praise is worth more than a ton of criticism."

Great care should be taken in handling decisions made by our children. There is no harm, and indeed only good, in our six year old saying they want to be a Christian and our accepting that at face value. However, an essential part of salvation is understanding the enormity of our sins and being genuinely repentant in front of the Lord. No six year old is able to grasp that fully, so we need to keep shepherding them sensitively so that, as their understanding matures, they can confirm their trust in Jesus, confess their sin and be assured of their salvation.

There is concern that decisions made at a very young age and not followed up can lead to a wishy-washy commitment and a genuine question about the actual validity of a person's faith. We are not the judge of an individual's position before God, although Jesus said we know His disciples by their fruit (Matthew 7:15-20). Maybe a reason for casual Christians in too many churches is a lack of anything more than 'accepting Christ.' No contrition?

Field 2 - Community

The second area in which we should be involved and active is our community, both in church and in our life outside of church - our neighborhood, work, leisure time and daily contacts. It is easy to stay hidden in our homes, pull up to the driveway, open the garage door, wave to the neighbor, put the door back down, and we are home in our little sanctuary. We should be engaging regularly with our neighbors as we have the privilege of taking the name of Jesus to the lost.

Every day that we go to work has the potential to build deeper relationships with co-workers. When taking the time to build and develop friendships, we have greater opportunities to share about our lives and the impact of Christ in our lives. Living out our faith in the communities we find ourselves in daily isn't about doing something new, but about doing and being something fuller in Christ.

Field 3 - Nation

We need to have a love for our nation. Not many churches have the reach to impact the whole of our nation. Yet there is an important role for churches and evangelical organizations that have nationwide coverage. The postmodern era has undermined the vital role that Christianity plays in building our nation and influencing individuals toward Christ and the salvation He offers. We commend those who have a love for our country and are actively seeking to win the whole country for Christ. They deserve our support.

Part of our role is to pray that those who have governmental and business leadership roles will come to faith in Christ. Jesus told us that the greatest commandments can be summed up by loving God and loving people. It begins with our neighbors, communities, and nations. We are to respect and pray for those in positions of influence, that through their actions the Kingdom of God may advance in whatever place you call home. Paul wrote to the Romans, "Everyone must submit himself to the governing authorities, for there is no authority except that which God has established." (Romans 13:1). The authorities that exist have been established by God. We are to respect and obey those in government, as God has instituted these to help protect us.

Field 4 - The Wider World

The fourth mission field is often the most ignored. We must never overlook the needs of the millions that are underprivileged, in vulnerable situations, displaced, or in one of the more than six thousand people groups who have yet to hear the name of Jesus or who need to have the Bible in their own language. Much of the focus of this book is on this part of our mission field, for out there is the greatest need. Sadly, today missions is often neglected and forgotten. A lot of people believe out of sight, out of mind. Jesus has commanded His disciples to be willing to go to the ends of the earth (Acts 1:8).

Think of it this way. Your family, your neighbors, your fellow workers and colleague - in fact, all Americans - are almost certainly going to hear the gospel or have easy access to hearing it several times over their life. In this book, we are more concerned with those who haven't heard it and will not unless you and I do something about it.

The Structure of Missions: A Holistic Approach

At the beginning of Jesus' ministry, He gathered together some verses from Isaiah - the servant chapters - and used them to outline His ministry (see Luke 4:17-27). This comprehensive approach is aimed not only at dealing with the greatest needs of mankind, but points toward the mature and fulfilling life that Jesus sought for those who follow Him. We can do no better than copy His mission shown here.

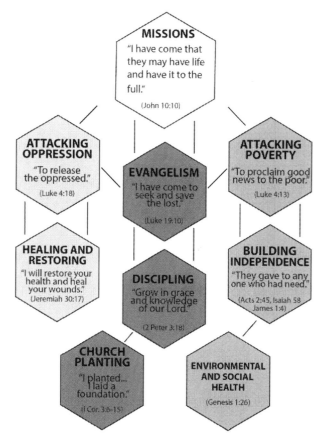

There is a huge need internationally to build depth as well as width in our missions' activity. The emphasis in Matthew 28 is the making of disciples, which is an ongoing role, baptizing and teaching, building converts up in the faith and knowledge of the Lord to become devoted followers. There is a need to see churches planted with a foundation of sound doctrine and an ability to take up the role of discipleship themselves.

John Stott accurately said, "Evangelicals have experienced enormous statistical growth … without corresponding growth in discipleship."[4] There are a huge number of young, enthusiastic pastors in India, for example, deeply committed to evangelism and church planting. That is hugely beneficial. The growing problem is that these young churches have no one to teach them sound doctrine and grow them into maturity in Christ. They need continuing discipling. Many churches in more remote places become unsound, falling back into their old ways of animism, Hinduism and dangerous occultist behavior, simply because they do not know better. There is no systematic discipleship.

Our western churches are generally not strategic enough. Many missions programs need better integrating into the whole church program, better organization, and a deliberate planned approach within the context of the local church. The church today needs more focus in its missions program on Romans 12:2, "Do not conform to the pattern of this world, but be transformed by the renewing of your mind" - something that can only occur by a closer interaction with God's Word. The aim for all of us is a growing maturity in Christ, as it says in James 1:4, "… so that you may be mature and complete, not lacking anything." We are commanded to make disciples and mobilize disciples to impact the world with the love and message of Jesus Christ.

This basic information sets the scene for this book. If you've made it this far, you will have a feel for where we are heading and what the main messages are going to be. Next, we want to share a little about what the Bible says about missions, because that is our authority and guidebook.

REACQUAINT
CHAPTER REFLECTIONS

INDIVIDUALS

PRAY

1. Spend time on your knees asking God to ignite a deeply rooted passion for missions in your life, family and church. May this be the first step of many toward living on mission for God.
2. Spend time on your knees for the Holy Spirit to speak to you and to reveal to you through the Bible what the Scripture says about missions.
3. Spend time on your knees asking for opportunities to personally disciple someone, and continue the cycle from Jesus to the apostles.

ENGAGE

1. Spend time this week looking up what the Bible has to say about missions, discipleship, and evangelism. Write down what you discover about God's heart for the nations and Jesus' call and commands for His disciples regarding evangelism.
2. Seek out missionaries you know of and spend time learning about their mission work and how you can be involved.
3. Spend time this week learning about unreached people groups. A great website is joshuaproject.net.

GO

1. Get your family on mission and seek out families in your neighborhood or community that you could serve right now.
2. Seek out ways for you and your family to serve your local community regularly.

CHURCHES

PRAY

1. Spend time on your knees seeking how your church can transform and engage families in your local community.
2. Spend time on your knees asking how your people can be embedded into the life of the local and global community and make these ministries part of your DNA.
3. Spend time on your knees asking how you can be involved globally sharing Jesus.

ENGAGE

1. Does your church have a healthy balance of the four mission fields: family, local community, nation, and world? Is there one you are more focused on? If so, why? What may need to change?
2. Is your church effective in making disciples and mobilizing them for mission daily?
3. In what ways can you cultivate a culture of sending and deploying disciples in your church?

GO

1. How are you creating opportunities for your people to be involved in serving within your church, and within the local and global community?

2. Create opportunities outside of the walls of your church where you can strategically partner with missions organizations and missionaries where your members can engage with living on mission for God.

CHAPTER 2

REVIEW

What does the Bible say about missions?

"To know the will of God, we need an open Bible and an open map."
— William Carey

"The Bible is not the basis of missions; missions is the basis of the Bible."
— Ralph Winter, Missiologist

God is a missionary God. He always has been, right from the beginning - and He always will be. He has always sought to have a people in which He can shower His love and reflect His glory. He did that with His people, Israel: He is doing it today with His church, and throughout eternity, the saved will honor and glorify Him.

In this chapter, we'll look at several examples from the Old and New Testaments which will help us understand the Bible's basis for missions.

In Genesis 3:8, after Adam and Eve had disobeyed God, the Lord God was walking in the garden seeking their fellowship. He is committed to seeking us even when we have cut ourselves off from Him through disobedience as Adam and Eve did. He has the best in mind for you and me. He is so dedicated to our needs and has such a desire to reach us that He does whatever it takes to get us back together again.

The Lord God took an animal and sacrificed it so Adam and Eve could be clothed. It pointed to the great sacrifice of His beloved Son at Calvary so that we all might have the opportunity to be clothed in righteousness and glory.

The Bible is a missions' book from the table of contents to the maps in the back. God is a missionary God seeking the lost, restoring His people and offering forgiveness. The Old Testament is filled with God declaring His glory to the nations. God is a missionary and continually wants to send people out in His name and for His glory.

The same plan remains from the beginning until today. God called out Abram, changed his life and his name, then used him to create a new nation of people for His glory. Abraham was an ordinary man who had a mighty relationship with God and there is much to learn from him: his faith and trust, his

---

God – Missional From the Very Beginning

Even before Adam and Eve, God established the pattern of His missional aims. The creation record, which is sadly such a maligned and controversial story, is more about God's nature and missional aims than it is about recording history.

What was "without form and void" was brought to life by the Holy Spirit and became something productive and beautiful. Light entered and the fruit of God's work became evident. God called on Adam and Eve to "be fruitful and multiply" (Genesis 1:28).

His message remains the same. That which is unproductive is brought to new life by the Spirit. We are to follow in Adam and Eve's footsteps by going out and multiplying new lives in Christ.

role as progenitor of God's chosen people, his implicit obedience. He is an excellent example of those who were ready to answer God's call whatever the cost.

Moses – A Challenging Example

When the children of Israel were lost in Egypt, Moses eventually followed the command of the Lord God and went and rescued them. He was the one who brought them new beginnings in a land of milk and honey. Moses is an interesting example of how God works and we don't. Can you imagine the C.V. Moses had covering his early life? He had a charmed beginning as a result of a clever, concerned mother who hid him from the vengeful Pharaoh. She shrewdly set herself up as his nurse and caregiver and even got paid to do it. Moses was raised as a prince in the palace of the most powerful and wealthy king of his time. Clearly he spent time in the gym and such were his skills that he could take on an Egyptian who would have, as a minimum, a whip, and dispatch him bare-handedly.

Somehow, his heroics got to the great Pharaoh's ear and he set out to kill Moses. It would have taken more than luck to escape this ruthless, barbaric leader. Moses took off for Midian, hundreds of miles away and across the Red Sea. This was good preparation for what was to come many years later. Midian was a tough, cruel place, almost devoid of vegetation and any rain. The people who lived there adapted, but it developed a ruggedness and independence that was to help turn the palace boy into a doughty leader.

In Midian, people stayed close to a well. It was vital for survival, but also the place where they meet the locals. The next scene from Exodus 2:16 is the stuff of movies. It doesn't take much imagination. Seven young ladies, the daughters of a priest and a farmer, arrived at the well to fill their water pots and supply

Your 'Burning Bush'

Life is comfortable. Nice home, happy relationships, good family, enjoyable job with promotion opportunities, mortgage coming down, replaced the car, and great church with satisfying worship.

Then WHAM! Out of the blue, after spending time in God's Word, you feel a powerful presence of God and a clear call to serve Him. It may be reinforced in a sermon, reading alone, at a men's group, or simply driving down the highway, preparing for the evening's BBQ, or lying awake one night.

The call from Christ to "go" comes to you unmistakably. What to do? It is easy to kill it. Just get busy and distracted with something else. It will fade. Or, maybe …

drink for their sheep and goats. Watching was this newly bronzed young stranger with a handsome physique. Can't you hear the chatter, giggling and banter? Who was going to make the first move?

The decision was made for them. Some hooligan shepherds arrived, jealous over the water supply, and they tried to drive these seven, young maidens away - but Moses was up to it. You can imagine the scene. The superb, trained athlete against the ragtag shepherds. A few quick blows and the cowardly shepherds were gone. Moses, now the gentleman, keen to impress, fetched the water for the girls. It was all a bit much for them. Overcome by shyness, they ran for home. Their father enquired how it was they were home so early. Again, imagine the scene as seven girls were falling over each other, all talking over one another trying to describe the rescue and tell their father about the handsome stranger who even drew the water they needed.

Their father rightly asked why they didn't ask him home for some desert hospitality. He probably figured he could find a husband for at least one of his daughters. What fun - seven girls going back to find their new hero and ask him for a meal. If you were Moses, would you say "no?" Of course not. The desert is an unforgiving place and not a place to be homeless or on one's own.

What a win for Moses - he gets a roof over his head (probably a goatskin), he gets a job and he gets a wife. All seems fine. A son is born and Moses has his feet well and truly under the table. Forty years pass. Did Moses let his fitness - both spiritual and physical - slip? Where were his heart and mind when God came calling? The Lord God, Yahweh, had plans, and the plan did not involve Moses growing old in the land of Midian working for his father-in-law.

In one of those well-known Sunday school stories that we learned as kids, the Lord appeared to Moses in a burning bush that was not consumed - an unusual miracle (Exodus 3:2). Yahweh called Moses from the bush and shared His heart for His people back in Egypt. "I hear their cries," the Lord told him. "I am sending you to Pharaoh to bring my people out of Egypt and into a land flowing with milk and honey."

Moses was far from impressed. He had settled into a sweet life with his wife and family, his home and job. He objected. "Who am I that you should ask me?" he whines. "Who will I say sent me?" More excuses. "What if they don't believe me?"

Moses wasn't going to give in easily. "Lord, I am not a very convincing speaker. I am no orator." Yahweh batted away his excuses one by one. As a last resort Moses demanded "Anyone but me Lord. Can't you find someone else for the job?"

Your Response May Be:

"I have no money to put into missions." Nor did Peter, James, John or Andrew. God is not asking for money.

"I have no time to put into missions." You think fishing was not time demanding?

"I have no calling." It is not based on a calling. It is a command – yes, a command – for everyone, no exceptions.

"It is too difficult." Yeah, so was the cross. So was being crucified upside down as Peter was.

"My church is doing it." Great. However, Jesus was not addressing churches with the Great Commission – he was addressing individuals.

"My life is a good witness – isn't that enough?" Excellent, great start. Now you have some runs on the board and the 99 are safely in the fold. Let's go after the 100th lost sheep as Christ did.

"I might end up in some rough place like India." What a privilege that would be. A crown awaits those who suffer while serving Christ. However, you can be just as effective at home doing what you are doing now and still be in missions in India.

I must say, when I hear how Moses reacted, it rings a familiar bell for me. How often has the Lord spoken from His Word and I have felt that call to be His servant, only to find a heap of excuses and suggest there are others better equipped for the task. I am not just referring to the once only call that some may receive to dedicate the rest of their life to Christ's service, but the everyday calls He makes of us to serve Him. I know I have found a way of turning down that small voice of the Holy Spirit when He has made plain His desire for me.

Is that where you are? Have you done a 'Moses' when God puts a task in front of you, even a small task where little sacrifice is involved? Have you found a way of extinguishing that call, that request, snuffing out the Lord's voice? You may not have seen the Lord in a burning bush or heard His voice audibly, but you know in your heart that He has made His requests very clear in His Word, and you also know you have brushed Him away with excuses. Today is a good time to stop and put matters right. Get back into His Word and plead for Him to make you aware of His voice and His desires for you, whether they are big, life changing requests, or the smaller everyday steps of obedience needed to be in fellowship with Him. He can only make His voice heard when we are in His Word reading, meditating, seeking, praying, listening and have a heart ready to put aside excuses and respond positively.

Yahweh was remarkably patient with Moses. He listened to all the excuses Moses came up with and patiently batted them away until Moses went a step too far. The Bible says the Lord is "slow to anger." It doesn't say He never gets angry. Ultimately, the righteousness and holiness of the Almighty must be satisfied. He changes His tone from asking to demanding, and Moses realizes he is losing against the sheer majesty of Yahweh, so he acquiesces. God's work will be done - we either do it graciously, or we miss out on the fullness of His blessing as Moses did by having God appoint Aaron alongside him.

Consider these points about the call of Moses and the excuses he used:

- Yahweh Himself spoke to Moses from the burning bush. Hebrews 1:2 tells us He still speaks through the Word, the One who became flesh and dwelt among us. Have you ever stopped to consider that incredible truth? He, the great I AM, wants to speak to us, address us by name and call us to serve Him.

- Yahweh sets out in detail His plans for His hurting people and how Moses was part of the plan. In a similar way, God graciously sets out His plans for the lost and hurting today. He nominates us to be part of that plan. He is sending us. He wants us to take a planned approach too.

- Yahweh could have stretched out His hand and in one miraculous gesture scooped His needy people from Egypt and transferred them to the chosen land. However, He chooses to use His own children - at least, the obedient ones. He is relying on you and me to reach the needy. Devoted disciples are the only messengers He has. It's also about our spiritual journey and God being glorified in our obedience and growth.

- The first excuse Moses offered was simple. "Who am I, that I should be asked to do this?" How many times have you and I resorted to such an excuse? Asked to help with a task at church, asked to join a Christian coffee club, asked to help pick up kids after a church event, asked to speak about our faith at a work function, asked to distribute flyers for a special church event, asked to go on a short term mission trip, asked to join the deacons, asked to take up a new ministry or asked to go to the mission field for a period of years, and you stand on your dignity with a "Why me?" Summed up, it's a form of inverted pride.

> ## Working for the Boss of all Bosses
>
> Sometimes I think our missions efforts are crippled by a lack of understanding of who employs us. Imagine if you were called tomorrow to work for the President as his close support person. If POTUS said, "all the resources of my office are at your disposal and I want you to do a really good job," would you mess around doing only what you wanted? Would you ignore the opportunity to use all the means open to the President?
>
> Maybe if our appreciation of the Lord God Almighty and His storehouse of mercy and grace were to grow and develop, we would be a little more committed.

The First Excuse

Yahweh had already told Moses in Exodus 3:8 that He was going to be the One who delivered His people. All the resources of the Godhead were going to be deployed for this task. When we say to the Lord, "Who am I, that I should be asked?" we are actually saying we don't trust Him to give us the strength and grace to do the task. We are belittling the Almighty. The very last message from Jesus to His disciples before He departed was that they would receive power from the Holy Spirit. That message is just as true today.

Nepal Trip

A few years ago, I (Owen) was out in a village in Nepal over 12 hours from Kathmandu. We ran out of bottled water - not a good idea, as it was over 105 degrees Fahrenheit. I drank the local polluted water to survive, but became horribly ill with vomiting and diarrhea. To get back, we had to walk for a couple of hours then catch a bus for the long trip back to Kathmandu. It was a dreadful trip, stopping to use the lavatory when there was not even a bush for cover, sitting on a wooden bus seat hemmed in by locals with their hens, goats, and assorted animals, and arriving in Kathmandu at 9:00p.m. A whole group of people waited at our partner's house to hear the visitor share the Word of God. It simply was not humanly possible. "Who am I that I should be asked?" went through my mind. "Not I, but Christ" the Holy Spirit flooded my mind. Sermons in Nepal last an hour or they are dismissed as lightweight. I placed myself in the Lord's hands and began reading the first chapter of Ephesians. The Holy Spirit fulfilled His promise.

The Second Excuse

The second excuse Moses made was, "What shall I say?" (Exodus 3:11-13). It's a common excuse. I would like to witness, I would like to go on a mission trip, I would like to go to the church golf match with an unsaved friend BUT, "What shall I say?" We feel embarrassed or we don't know how to turn a conversation about the weather or the football game to an arresting question about a friend's soul.

Yahweh's response is gracious. Simply tell them what you know. Jesus' message was that we should be witnesses. A witness tells what they have experienced. We simply give a reason for the changes we know that have happened in our own lives. "All I can say is that I read that Jesus came into the world to save sinners, died and rose again, and since I trusted in Him, my life has changed." That is pretty easy.

One of our hang-ups is that we think God wants us to save people. He doesn't. In fact, we can't save people. Only God can.

We simply sow the seed. The Holy Spirit germinates the seed, waters it, and brings the change and growth. Stop trying so hard. Stop worrying about what to say. The Lord promises the words in Exodus 4:12 and it is He who does the heavy lifting.

Another obstacle that can form in our minds is that the world is populated by millions who are lost. "Where will I start?" "What can I possibly say that will make a difference among so many needy?" "What I can say or do will not make any difference in such vast numbers." When we face this obstacle we forget the power of compounding. If we witnessed to one person every month who came to know Christ as their Savior, and the new believers did the same, the world would be won for Christ in less than four years. Less than four years. It is a sad commentary on the weakness of our efforts and our lack of faith and obedience.

Secondly, when we feel overwhelmed with where to start, we would do well to remember that one life transformed by the gospel is a matter of great importance. Not only is it an eternally life-changing moment to that person, but for those already in glory there is rejoicing over one sinner repenting (Luke 15:7). It is the starfish effect. An old man and his grandson were walking on the beach after a storm. Thousands of dying starfish had been thrown up by the merciless waves. The boy carefully picked one up and threw it back. The old man said, "You are wasting your time. You can't make a difference to this lot." The boy's response was priceless: "Ah, but it will make a difference for this one."[5] Don't be paralyzed by the sheer numbers: focus on what God has asked of you.

The Third Excuse

Moses' third excuse to God is centered on a fear of failure. "What if they don't believe me? What if they don't listen? What if they reject me? What if I fail?" (Exodus 4:1) Fear of failure and rejection are huge obstacles for us. By becoming more insular and self-focused we can avoid "outside" interaction that can bring failure or loss. By living for ourselves we can control more of what happens around us. We have become a very 'me-focused' society. If it doesn't suit 'me' or if it threatens 'me' I won't go there.

The life that Christ calls us to is very, very different. It is all about sacrifice and the needs of others. Take the example of Jesus. He was wholly focused on the cross. He came to die. He came to do not His will and what suited Him, but to do His Father's will. He was totally focused on our needs as sinners and went through unspeakable agony and loss for us. His call to us is to follow His example. Read Philippians 2 for a great example of countering the self-centered society we live in.

The scary thing is that this selfishness has caught on in our churches and among Christians today. We are being more cocooned from a world of sacrifice and serving others. 'Me-ism' demands instant gratification at the expense of all else. Even in our churches we want shortcuts to blessings. It is not just the excesses of the prosperity doctrine which is creating a paucity of "riches in Christ," but, seductively and in typical sinister fashion, pastors are falling to "the itching ears." When Paul wrote his second letter to Timothy, he said that the time would come when "men will not put up with sound doctrine. Instead, to suit their desires, they will gather round them a great number of teachers to say what their itching ears want to hear" (2 Timothy 4:3).

Yes, we want to be Christians. We want to attend church most Sundays too, but don't give us this hard stuff about sacrifice and missions, witnessing and giving ourselves for the cause of Christ. We want the easy stuff, secure that we have a ticket to heaven, but unwilling to face the demands of what the Bible calls dying to self and putting on Christ.

Conversation – A Dying Art

I picked up my grandson from football practice the other night. He grunted something, threw his gear in the back seat and promptly started texting on his phone. I waited a bit and asked him how practice went. Silence. Thumbs were in overdrive. After a minute I got an "Okay, Pop." The flying thumbs resumed. I tried again. Another pause. Another sullen answer as though I was encroaching on something vital.

I pulled off on the side of the road a long way from home. He didn't notice for a bit, then asked, "What are we doing?" barely looking up from the screen. "You obviously don't need me," I said. "Hop out, there will be a bus along soon." He got the message and soon found his voice, sliding the phone into his pocket.

Modern technology is killing conversation. TV, phones, computers, and tablets are turning us into verbal hermits. What an opportunity for Christians. Let's reclaim conversation. Let's be known as those who talk to each other.

The Fourth Excuse

Moses had yet another excuse. This time, he tried to convince God that he was not an orator. He stammered and his speech was too incoherent. Yahweh's answer is priceless.

"The Lord said to him, 'Who gave human beings their mouths? Who makes them deaf or mute? Who gives them sight or makes them blind? Is it not I, the Lord?'" (Exodus 4:11). God was basically saying, "Moses, don't be an idiot. You're speaking to the Lord God, Creator of all things and Master of the universe. Fixing a speech problem, real or imagined, is a mere trifle." But you and I try pulling those excuses. We will run from anything to avoid facing up to the command of Christ to "go into all the world and share the gospel." Oratory is actually the last thing we need. Sincerity is the key, not fine-sounding words.

Finally, Yahweh's patience is stretched. Moses shows his true colors. The excuses were smokescreens. He simply did not want to do what the Lord God wanted. In Exodus 4 Moses says, "…Pardon your servant Lord. Please send someone else." Leave it to the pastor, elders or those who want to be missionaries. Just leave me be. Let the lost and poor wait. One by one, they slip into eternity without Christ because of disobedience and an unwillingness to take up our responsibilities.

I guess there is yet another excuse that Moses could have used. It is one that substantially weakens the modern church's mission efforts. Moses had grown comfortable right where he was. He had it made. A good job, a wife and kids, six beautiful sisters-in-law, and very agreeable in-laws. Forty years of peace suited him just fine. Only a couple of nagging things disturbed him. He had killed an Egyptian man, and he was aware his own people were still trapped in Egypt (Exodus 1:11).

Is that where you are right now? Most things are just fine. Life is OK. Your church meets your needs, you get a spiritual buzz each Sunday from a rousing service and a 'pick-me-up' sermon. There is just one nagging problem - the people around you and around the world are trapped in sin. They need someone to rescue them, but life is just too comfortable.

We have focused on Moses and even given him a little flak. In some ways, it's a bit unfair to condemn Moses. He was very human - much like you and me. It says a lot about the Lord's graciousness and forbearance that He arranged Aaron to be His helper and was to go on and make Moses one of the true greats of history. How many people can say they were the "friend of God?"

It is the same with you and me. God is willing to forgive our selfishness, our unwillingness to answer His call and our lukewarmness

"You Shall be My Witnesses"

As Christians we are all witnesses. If we have truly experienced repentance and grace, being born again by the Spirit, we have witnessed something. We have something to tell.

Jesus didn't say it was optional. We are either a good witness, a neutral witness or a bad witness. What messages are you conveying? What does the great court of public opinion think of your evidence contribution?

for evangelism and missions. There is time to put the excuses behind us and face the fact that we can do all things through Christ who strengthens us (Philippians 4:13). If this great, all-powerful, all-knowing God is for us, who can possibly be against us? (Romans 8:31). Today is the day to start.

How 'Me-ism' is Killing the Church and Missions

One of the biggest battles we face as Christians is with our own ego. Of all the activities in a church and in our Christian life, missions is the hardest and asks the biggest sacrifice. It takes a great deal of selflessness to do missions. Some of us struggle to really 'let go and let God.'

We like to have a buck both ways. I want to know I am going to heaven when I die and enjoy the fellowship and worship time at my church, but don't ask me to drop all my ambitions and desires for God's sake. It is a halfway house that the Lord finds distasteful. He said to the church in Laodicea, a town in what we now call Turkey, "I know your deeds, you are neither cold nor hot. I wish you were one or the other! But because you are lukewarm—neither cold nor hot—I am about to spit you out of my mouth!" (Revelation 3:15-16) Ugh! Not a nice position.

The believers in Laodicea knew exactly what He was talking about, because the city had invested in a huge pipeline to bring hot water to the city from an underground source several miles away. They figured they could construct baths for their recreational enjoyment. Unfortunately, the engineers got their calculations wrong, and the water was not hot enough to bathe in, but also too warm to drink. It was rather revolting. It was useless, and unfit for purpose. People just wanted to spit it out.[6] Jesus went on and said to the Laodiceans they needed to get real and be earnest. They needed to repent of the lukewarmness and open their whole life to Christ so their fellowship could be complete and effective (Revelation 3:16). Otherwise, He would spit them out of His mouth.

Sadly, many Christians are comfortable being lukewarm. 'Me-ism' has them firmly in its grasp. The attitudes around us in our society are tragically rubbing off on Christians. Social media has given every person a publishing platform seen around the globe. Suddenly an unknown, modest soul in any unknown town can be an internet sensation, glorified and feted by all and sundry. This is the ultimate appeal to ego. A recent survey of millennials found that most considered self-gratification more important than 'helping others.'[7]

Recently Josh McDowell, a Christian writer on trends in society, put it this way when commenting on the way many people see themselves:

- "There is nothing more important than the individual. I am self-sustaining and free from any authority I do not choose to follow."[8]
- "The highest of human values and experiences is personal satisfaction and pleasure. I am entitled to my share of pleasure and comfort."[9]
- "I must constantly be vigilant that my 'needs' will be met."[10]
- "The most important of loves is the love of self. Without this, I will be unable to function."[11]

This is the dead opposite of what Christ taught. When He said "Follow Me," His anticipation was that we would put Christ first, others next, and ourselves last. Consider these verses from Romans 12:1-2, "I urge you, in view of God's mercy, to offer yourselves as living sacrifices, holy and pleasing to God.... Do not be conformed to this world, but be transformed by the renewing of your minds..." Paul's message here is plain and clear.

Besides Paul's exhortation in Romans, we have this dramatic statement from Jesus: "If anyone comes to me and does not hate his father and mother, his wife and children, his brothers and sisters—yes, even his own life—he cannot be my disciple" (Luke 14:26). Extreme, you say? Jesus was making a strong point. He wants us 100% focused and committed. The cost of discipleship, of following Christ, of being committed to missions, is to be sold out on everything else except Him. He is entitled to ask that of us because He was utterly committed to us. He didn't pull back from Gethsemane or the cross. He didn't bother with distractions like a home, an 8-cylinder camel, a big screen TV or his own boat. Christ is seeking committed people. He rejects those who persist in 'me-ism.'

Jonah – A Doubtful Example

Jonah was given the task of taking a message to a needy people. I quite like Jonah. I remember having his story read to me as a young kid, all eyes and ears as I tried to contemplate getting swallowed by a whale and surviving three days in its stomach juices. It was a tough outcome for a guy who was only guilty of turning his back on God and refusing the call to go and be God's witness in Nineveh. Mind you, the Ninevites were Assyrians, and they were a tough bunch.

It was a relief to find that God was patient and gave Jonah a break. The second time, Jonah wasted no time in obeying Yahweh's instruction and off to Nineveh he went. I reckon that Jonah got the shock of his life when he stood up in Nineveh and said that great calamity would overtake the people of the wicked city if they didn't repent and turn to worship the one true God.

No sooner had Jonah followed Yahweh's call and the people responded, right up to the King. Poor and rich, young and old expressed their sorrow for their sins and their disobedience. Jonah couldn't believe what he was seeing. The whole city was turning to God. Instead of jumping for joy, Jonah got all churlish and angry. He couldn't believe that Yahweh, who had punished him for his disobedience, could shower such an evil city with grace and save them from destruction. Jonah got himself in a huff and went and sat outside the city waiting to see if God would withhold His righteous judgment.

The BIG 'I.' This was Jonah's problem. He was a 'me-ist.' Note how many times he focuses on himself in the four chapters of his book. Everything revolves around him, his feelings, his wants. If there is one thing that characterizes the modern world, it is selfishness and self-centeredness. The last few decades in particular have seen the swing towards 'me-ism' taking place at a faster rate. In the 1960's, we were encouraged to 'express ourselves,' 'develop our own personality' and 'give reign to our self-expression.' In many instances, this movement was helpful. Once upon a time children were seen and not heard. They were encouraged to speak only when spoken to. "Don't be pushy" my Mom used to say, or "remember your place." However, it has led to another extreme. Now it's all about me. Social media has worsened the situation by giving anybody and everybody worldwide attention - literally.

Elijah – A Bold Faith Example

Elijah was a messenger. He received instructions from God. In faith, he obeyed. God was seeking fellowship with His people, the nation of Israel, but they resolutely turned their back on Him. He sent Elijah to warn King Ahab. Ahab was totally off the rails, greatly influenced by his evil wife Jezebel. God's message was consistent. He told His people if they got their lives right through obedience to His message, He would bless them abundantly. On the other side of the coin was a warning - keep rejecting Me and expect punishment.

Imagine fronting up to a ruthless, dangerous king and his scheming queen to warn them of a major catastrophe befalling them if they continued to defy God - a three year drought. That took incredible courage and remarkable faith. You might be thinking that God will not call you to witness to a king, good or bad. Yet the same faith that Elijah demonstrated is available to you and me. Hebrews 11 and 12 tell us that it was ordinary men and women who did extraordinary things by faith.

The message is to fix your eyes on Christ as an example. Romans 10:17 explains that we access that type of faith from hearing, and that hearing is by the Word of God. There lies the key. We need to be constantly hearing the encouraging, instructive messages that come from God's book. When someone tells you they do not have the faith to do something, gently ask whether they are immersing themselves in the messages that God has for them in His Word.

Now, here is a great truth we learn from Elijah. By Chapter 19 of 1 Kings, Elijah is on the run. He has just humiliated the priests of Baal at Mount Carmel by showing there is only one true God. He receives word that Ahab and Jezebel are on the attack, and any prophet of God is the target. So naturally, Elijah flees for his life. He journeys out into the wilderness to flee from the dangers of Jezebel's threats. "The LORD said, 'Go out and stand on the mountain in the presence of the LORD, for the LORD is about to pass by.' Then a great and powerful wind tore the mountains apart and shattered the rocks before the LORD, but the LORD was not in the wind. After the wind there was an earthquake, but the LORD was not in the earthquake. After the earthquake came a fire, but the LORD was not in the fire. And after the fire came a gentle whisper. When Elijah heard it, he pulled his cloak over his face and went out and stood at the mouth of the cave" (1 Kings 19:11-13).

We often want God to turn up in a big and dramatic way. Sometimes He does. Mostly, He doesn't. There were three episodes that Elijah witnessed, thinking that God would be in them and he would hear from Him. Ever waited to hear God's voice? Ever been at your wits end hoping to see a glimpse of God? It is not fun listening to silence when you want to hear a voice. God wasn't in the wind, He wasn't in the earthquake or the fire - three powerful experiences that came before Elijah. Instead, God showed up through a gentle whisper.

How did Elijah discern that voice? How was Elijah about to hear? He had attuned his ears to the voice of the One who made him. The Almighty God of heaven and earth came not through power and might, but through a gentle whisper. If we are not careful, we will miss it. We will fail to hear God's voice. That's why reading His word, sitting back, and meditating on it is vital for hearing God speak.

Thoughts From the New Testament

All four gospels and the book of Acts focus heavily on Jesus' words of instruction, as He encouraged the early disciples to make it their mission to become more committed disciples themselves, and also to concentrate on making disciples among others. In order to be missional in our thinking and living, we must be committed disciples ourselves. The Lord also desires that we become passionate about the discipleship of others. While evangelism is an absolutely essential element in missions, it is not the full package. Missions is actually more about on-going discipleship than it is evangelism. To grow in our own walk with Jesus we need to live for His mission, daily committed to discipling as well as evangelism.

Being a disciple is not just about attending church once a week, or on the 'special' times throughout the year, like Christmas and Easter, putting some surplus cash in the offering plate once in a while, and volunteering once a year at Vacation

Bible School. Disciples live daily for the pursuit of following Christ and making disciples. They are totally committed. If we want to grow in our maturity as a disciple, we are to not only believe Jesus, but obey Him and join Him for His mission daily.

The new equation for global missions should be that missions = discipleship. We need to expand our view of missions from just being a process of reaching the unsaved and seeing them born again to being a lifelong commitment to grow ourselves and others into Christlikeness. We need that Pauline aspiration – "I consider everything a loss compared to the surpassing greatness of knowing Christ Jesus my Lord for whose sake I have lost all things. I consider them rubbish that I may gain Christ and be found in Him not having a righteousness of my own that comes from the law but that which is through faith in Christ - the righteousness that comes from God and is by faith. I want to know Christ and the power of His resurrection and the fellowship of sharing in His sufferings becoming like Him in His death and so, somehow, to attain to the resurrection from the dead" (Philippians 3:7-11).

Our good friends, we really want to impress on you the value in these verses when considering missions. If missions = discipleship, then we need to fully take on Paul's goals.

Note some of Paul's characteristics:

A.   It was all or nothing for Paul. The past was consigned to history: whatever he had believed, hoped for and trusted in previously was thrown overboard - gone, dead and buried. He was utterly and totally focused now on his disciple journey in Christ.

B.   His sole goal was now the greatness of Christ, knowing Him, understanding Him, obeying Him and being like Him.

C.   He was abandoning being an 'outward only' Christian, doing the things that were for show and that other people expected. He was done with trying hard to be righteous in his own strength (a.k.a. the 'me-ism' approach). Now he was going to live by faith alone, trusting Christ solely.

D.   He reckoned that "knowing Christ" was a top priority. He was going to immerse himself in understanding this Jesus as fully as possible so he could copy every trait and example.

E.   He figured that resurrection power was the path of victory. Not his own efforts, but tapping into the reservoir of energy the Father had demonstrated at the cross and resurrection (see Ephesians 1:19).

F.   He had figured out that in God's grand scheme of things, the pathway to blessing and effectiveness as a disciple lay in understanding the death of Christ as symbolic of reckoning the past dead, of even putting himself figuratively on a cross and dying so that he would be a new person completely, and in all respects ready to serve as a disciple. For Paul everything he had stood for, believed in, hoped for from his past that might have come between him and His Lord and Savior he rendered dead and buried. There were no half measures, no holding back but just bold determination to follow Jesus.

I don't know about you, but I am pretty gobsmacked by these verses. For much of my life, I tried to live in both worlds. We use expressions like 'having a foot in both camps,' or 'having it both ways.' We want to follow Jesus, but we have our own agenda, our own goals and aspirations. Being an effective disciple and being effective disciplers means that we are to follow Christ's and Paul's examples. When we try to get our minds around the enormity of our sin, the extent of the mercy of God, the size of His grace, the love of Jesus and His willingness to die for us, then emotionally we can surrender and offer Him our all. But will we carry that commitment forward every day, through thick and thin, through hardship and trial, through good days and bad days? That is why Paul made those somewhat odd statements like "I die daily" (1 Corinthians 15:31). Paul needed to deal every day with what would keep him from being an effective disciple. Proverbs 8:34 says, "Blessed is the man who listens to me, watching daily at my gates, waiting at my doorposts" (NASB).

Scene – Encounters

When Val met Jenny in the supermarket, she knew she needed to stop and talk. She really didn't have time, because she wanted to get her hair done later in the afternoon.

Something made her stop and talk. Jenny seemed a bit distant, a bit ruffled, and clearly not herself. They didn't know each other well but Jenny seemed to be enjoying the contact. Val looked at her watch trying to figure out how long she had before she could back out of the conversation.

To her surprise, Val found herself suggesting they have a coffee after checking out. "Oh bother," she thought, "now I am getting trapped." Jenny eagerly took her up on the tentative suggestion. They walked across to the coffee house.

To Val's surprise, Jenny had a lot to say. She opened up to having problems with her 15 year old son who was proving difficult to parent and a 12 year old daughter becoming unmanageable. Her mother-in-law was frustrating her by chipping in with advice all the time and she found Terry, her husband, backing his mother rather than her. Val gulped. "Why am I listening to all of this?"

Then the bombshell. Just when Val's thoughts had wandered back to the social hour she was going to be badly prepared for,

Jenny said, "Val, I can't help seeing how relaxed you are with your kids. They are so appreciative of you and David. You have a happiness that we can't seem to find. What's your secret?"

"Oh, my goodness," thought Val. "This is it. I am supposed to say something helpful. I am supposed to witness about my faith in Christ." Her hands shook a little while she tried to sort out the jumble of thoughts in her head. "I can't do this." "Yes, you can." "I don't know what to say." "Yes, you do." "I will sound like an idiot." "No, you will be okay - you know My promises." "She will laugh at me." "No, she is seeking help and you have answers." Val played for time. "I didn't know you knew too much about our family, Jenny," she offered. "Well, I have been noticing for some time now, and I have been looking for an opportunity to catch up and talk. Our problems are getting worse, not better."

Val drew a big breath. "We have similar problems, Jenny. You are not alone in your battles and we wish we could do better. It is not a secret as such - it's more that we have an extra person in our family who we rely on and who is always listening and helping. He is our unseen guest. You see, we invited Jesus into our lives a few years ago and we make Him part of our family. It doesn't make the problems go away, but it sure helps us in our relationships."

"Oh," Jenny said, clearly a little disappointed in the response. "How can a make-believe person who was supposed to have been here all those years ago help you now? I thought you might have some practical ideas."

"All I can do is tell you what happened to us and how it has made a difference in our lives. As I said, we are no different to anyone else and we have our difficult moments, but our relationships with each other, including mine with David, is ever so much better since we became Christians and made God's

Word, the Bible, part of our lives. We find praying together helps draw us together and creates a better atmosphere in our home. If you would like to know more about this, I am very friendly with our pastor's wife and she is more experienced than me. I will give you her cell number and I know she would love to talk to you. I just know it would help you."

Later, after Jenny had gone home, she kept getting the phone number out and looking at it, wondering if there was something to what Val had said. She had seemed to be so sincere and open about it. There was no doubt something was making a difference in Val's family. She reached for her phone and began dialing.

Ready, Set, Go

Paul said, "I die daily." He needed to face the practical reality that temptation was all around him, that his resolve to live for Christ in the power of the cross was vulnerable, that it wouldn't take much to unsettle him. He needed to go back every single day to his decision to put to death his own ambitions. He knew to be a disciple of Jesus he had to count every distraction and detraction as rubbish and stay focused on 'knowing the greatness of Christ.' How did he do that?

There is only one way to do that. The place to go to 'know the greatness of Christ' is in His Word, the Bible. That book is the revealing of Christ. From cover to cover it explains Him, uncovers His wonder, His beauty, His magnificence, His power and His plan. It is wonderfully described in the front of the Gideon Bibles and New Testaments:

"The Bible contains the mind of God, the state of man, the way of salvation, the doom of sinners, and the happiness of believers. Its doctrines are holy, its precepts are binding, its histories are true, and its decisions are immutable. Read it to be wise, believe it to be safe, and practice it to be holy. It contains light to direct you, food to support you, and comfort to cheer you.

"It is the traveler's map, the pilgrim's staff, the pilot's compass, the soldier's sword, and the Christian's charter. Here Paradise is restored, Heaven opened, and the gates of hell disclosed.

"Christ is its grand subject, our good the design, and the glory of God its end.

"It should fill the memory, rule the heart, and guide the feet. Read it slowly, frequently and prayerfully. It is a mine of wealth, a paradise of glory, and a river of pleasure. It is given you in life, will be opened at the judgment, and be remembered forever. It involves the highest responsibility, will reward the greatest labor, and will condemn all who trifle with its sacred contents."

When the letter to the Romans says we need to be "transformed by the renewing of our minds," it means we need to feed our minds - an on-going need. Our

A Gentle Man

We don't hear the word 'gentle' much these days, do we? When did you last hear someone described as 'gentle'? My Dad was gentle, never lost his temper, was kind, placid, tender-hearted, softly spoken, always thoughtful and sweet-spirited. Yet he was as hard as nails, resilient, persistent and rocklike. We used to go hiking and he was first to the hut, had lit the fire, made a billy of tea, helped carry someone else's pack. When disaster struck, he was the first line of defense. He never wilted.

The problem is we mistake gentleness for weakness when it is the opposite. It is a fruit of the Spirit. It is a stunning way to live—a powerful testimony.

minds do not operate in a vacuum. If we feed our minds rubbish, rubbish will come out. If we feed our minds on God's Word, our lives will be transformed and good things will emerge. The pithy saying that "sin keeps me from the Word of God and God's Word keeps me from sin" is so very true. The Psalmist said he had hidden God's Word in his heart so he wouldn't sin against the Lord (Psalm 119:11).

The Necessity of Prayer

Alongside immersing ourselves in the Word of God is the need to pray. For many years, I had simply believed that if I set aside a little time and prayed to the Father that I was doing what was needed. I would try and praise the Lord for His greatness and goodness, and then run through a list of things I thought were suitable requests to put to the Lord. I prayed for my family, for friends, for my church, for the missions I was interested in, for witnessing opportunities, for my business and for any special items of the day. It was a daily ritual and there was absolutely nothing wrong with it, except it meant I was missing out on a whole dimension of prayer.

If we go to the 13th chapter of John's gospel through to the end of chapter 17, we find Jesus enters into a very intimate and meaningful discourse with His disciples. He shuts out everything else to just focus on them. He wants to take them through intense detail on how to be an ideal disciple. Why? The reason is because to be an effective discipler, one needs to be an effective disciple. If this rough, tough small team were going to carry the can for changing the world, they better have some in-depth training and tuition.

This book isn't the place to run a detailed exegesis on these most important verses, except to comment on a few things vital to missions. It begins with Jesus washing His disciples' feet. I don't know about you, but I am not at all excited about washing someone else's feet. Who knows where they have been? It's pretty humiliating. And that is exactly what Jesus wanted His disciples to know. Discipling is humbling. It involves putting aside our pride. If you want to be a disciple of Jesus and make disciples of others, you have to learn to deal with pride.

I have watched Christians from wealthy countries arrive in the poorest of poor areas of the undeveloped world, and treat the local people with a lack of dignity and respect – a product of pride. It has been one of the most destructive things on the mission field. It is not about 'us' and 'them,' as we are all part of the body of Christ, though different members. We disciple in love, grace and humility. We bow and meet the needs of those in greatest needs by being their servant.

The Necessity of Love

In the latter part of John 13, Jesus lays down the big ask. Not just a suggestion or even a request. It is a command, a military term that cannot be disobeyed. "A new command I give you. Love one another" (John 13:34). We are to love one another as Christ loved - sacrificially, wholeheartedly, graciously, without discrimination or favor, with only the best in mind for others.

Love is such a maligned word today. Too often, it is reduced to a mindless, throwaway, meaningless insanity. The love of Christ and of the Bible that we need to wrap our minds around is a love for the sake of the person loved, that seeks only the best or the highest good for them - that is, not a feeling, but a deliberate, calculated commitment, whatever the cost. It is the very opposite of the "love you," "love my dog," "love chocolate," "if you love me you will…" nonsense that is all about me and what I want.

Loving others is hard work. It takes grit. It involves foregoing, missing out, hurting, humiliation, ridicule, even persecution, but the rewards are out of this world, literally. No matter what difficulties we may face, Paul reminds the church in Rome: "Yet what we suffer now is nothing compared to the glory He will reveal to us later" (Romans 8:18, NLT). If you and I are going to be making disciples, we need huge doses of this brand of love.

John chapter 14 begins with a little section about heaven. Don't you appreciate this comfort, grace and gentleness from Jesus? His disciples were going to face traumatic times, so the Master discipler takes time to share with them the ultimate comfort. He tells His disciples to not be troubled - no need to worry, as all we need to do is trust. Even in the darkest of days we can rely on Him and He will provide for us. Jesus explains that He is going to prepare a place that they can call home (John 14:1-3). One of the sweetest words to the human heart is the word 'home,' and Jesus reminds us when we follow Him, we will live with Him in the home prepared just for us, forever.

Some of us need to take more time to be gracious, thoughtful and responsive in a loving, gentle way. We live in a society that too often rewards toughness, brusqueness and excessive manliness. A little thoughtful grace goes a long way to preparing people around you to hear and respond to the gospel. By verse 15 of Chapter 14 Jesus has introduced a whole new idea. He tells His team not to fret, and that He was going off to heaven to get a place ready for them, but that He was sending the Holy Spirit to be alongside them.

He will be your Counselor, Comforter, Guide and Instructor. We are not alone as we go about making disciples. God, through

His Spirit, is within us, ever present, ever helping. I don't know about you, but I still cannot fully get my mind around this concept, even after years of being a Christian. Our great and mighty God not only deigns to save us by grace, but also comes and makes His home with us - there to help, comfort, convict, and guide. It is just tremendous truth.

You really have to love this next section in Chapter 15. I always imagine as they went out they passed under a very fruitful grapevine loaded with juicy grapes. Jesus stops. He uses the grapevine to teach them important truths about being a disciple and about discipling. There is too much for us to cover here, but a couple of quick points. Fruit bearing is an expected part of discipleship (verse 8). The key is staying close to the Father and the Son by hearing their words from Scripture, meditating on them, obeying them, and praying.

If you want to know real, lasting joy as opposed to temporary happiness, then follow the command to love one another. Serving Christ may be tough going and require persistence and patience, but it brings unmistakable joy that cannot be compared. Seeing unbelievably poor Hindu women transformed by the gospel, growing in Christ, becoming disciples brings joy beyond belief. Travelling down a dangerous road and getting horribly sick is nothing compared to getting there and seeing the look of gratitude on the faces in the village as fresh, clean water runs from a pipe for the first time. Seeing teens brave enough to stand up in front of their questioning peers to signify their willingness to accept God's salvation after hearing you speak is a joy that is hard to match. Watching young pastors' faces as they learn new ideas for running young people's camps and practice techniques for growing their people in Christ is a source of deep satisfaction. You will not find joy to come anywhere near that outside of making disciples.

The Necessity of Suffering

The next section is tough going. Jesus tells them that as His disciples, they are going to get persecuted. It certainly happened. Peter ended his life being crucified upside down. Early church writings suggest that at least seven of the disciples were martyred.

Jesus wanted them to learn a very basic Biblical truth. True happiness and blessing comes by way of a hard road. It is a difficult idea to grasp and make your own. Naturally, we want to be happy. We want instant and continuing happiness. We seek all manner of different ways to be happy, but most are transient, mercurial and unsatisfying.

What God offers is joy. He skipped 'happy.' He was into something much more valuable. He said through the Psalmist that "joy comes in the morning." Joy comes after the night and sometimes the night is very dark, lonely and long. When joy comes, we can appreciate it ever so much more because it contrasts with the pain of the night. Joy and grace are interrelated: we truly have joy when we understand the meaning of grace. Grace is a gift we receive from God, and this should translate into joy as we truly understand what we have been given. Experience life in all its abundance.

I (Owen) had the privilege of being present when our first baby was born. I watched helplessly as my wife went through hours of excruciating pain. Her cries were heart rending, her face bathed in perspiration as she fought through the agony. And then suddenly, a little baby arrived and was thrust into her arms. I shall never forget the look of sheer joy as she looked down on the tiny life she had brought into the world. The joy was so much more intense and cherished because it had been won by immense, physical pain.

Adding a Little to a True Story

I (Owen) am not sure whether we should make up stories like this, because we are not altogether certain on the detail of what heaven will be like. We actually do not need to know, because knowing Christ will be there is sufficient.

However, I like to muse on this: it concerns my daughter, who lost the delight of her life—her only child—in tragic circumstances. A shocking and anguished time in her life. Imagine she arrives in heaven. Jesus calls her over and wraps His arms around her shoulders. "My dear daughter. You don't know what it meant to Me when I was on the cross that your pain was shared by Me and My pain was shared by you. You 'participated in my sufferings' and I am eternally grateful. I too felt your anguish and walked every inch of your journey with you, heard every cry of pain and felt those hot, frustrating tears on your cheeks. I have a special place just for you, a place of unfathomable joy. Enter into your joy and eternal rest."

The most harrowing and unthinkably agonizing of all experiences came at the cross for Jesus. The Father God meted out on His own beloved Son the punishment for our sin. But Hebrews 12 tells us He did it for the "joy set before Him." The Father welcomed Him to His lofty position at His right hand. The "joy" goes forward as in a coming day God's purposes will be "put into effect and all things will be placed under Christ" (Ephesians 1:10–22).

The pattern was established. Pain and persecution leads to unbelievable joy. The purpose? That we may know joy in greater depth. That Christ may know we are prepared as His disciples to suffer for His account. James even said we should count it pure joy if we face trials of many kinds (James 1:2). He suggested it was part of our development toward maturity. Peter reckoned we should not be surprised by painful trials. He said we should rejoice in such happenings, because we are "participating in the sufferings of Christ" (1 Peter 4:13)

These are deep and difficult verses to comprehend fully, and it will be eternity before we know the reason in full. My (Owen) daughter and her partner have just lost their only child - a dear wee boy of nearly three years. They are unable to have more children so their agony and loss is still very raw. With us as grandparents, they are calling out to God in anger and disbelief that one so young and precious should be wrenched from their care. How could this happen? Why has it happened? There are no answers here, and maybe not in eternity. We are reaching into the depths of our faith to cope. Yet, as the days pass, so does the pain, and we realize our frailty and vulnerability. We are but grass in the field, sometimes cut down so young and tender. We lean more fully on the Comforter.

Like gold in the crucible and molten iron in the furnace, the greater the heat, the more pure the final product. As disciples, we trust that God is in control and He knows and loves us. If we are going to make disciples that are in themselves able to disciple others, the flame of trial needs to refine us and purify us. For wisdom from the Scriptures on these matters, see James 1:2 and 1:12, 1 Peter 4:12-19 and Romans 8:17-27. Ultimately nothing, no matter how grim and painful, can separate believers from Jesus (Romans 8:35). He comforts us like no other (2 Corinthians 1:3-4).

The last point we make is from John 17:13 to the end of the chapter. This is really amazing stuff. Jesus is praying for His disciples and for those who will be made disciples down through time. His prayer is for our joy to be full, that we may be protected from the evil one, that we might be sanctified, that there may be unity among disciples, that our witness will be effective so that the world may believe, that we will all one day be with Jesus, glorifying Him, and that the Father's love will be in us along with the Spirit of Christ. Wow! How about that? Jesus is backing you and me 100% as His disciples. He is burdened in prayer for us. He is calling on the Father on our behalf—imagine that. What better and more effective advocate could we have? That is very special.

If you are keen to be a good disciple and follow the command to make disciples of others, then make these four chapters of John your guide and encouragement. It is an ideal section of God's Word for instruction.

Story - What Opportunity?

Don was feeling upbeat. He had been asked to attend a course at the head office of his company and he knew it was the wrapping for a more serious present involving promotion and extra pay. He was to drive to the company headquarters with Steve, a four hour drive, on the day before the course began. He didn't know Steve all that well, despite meeting him and his wife a few times socially. The word around Don's office was that Steve could probably teach him a good deal about his new promotion position.

Steve drove the rental and they spent the first hour getting to know each other's background and role in the company. Don was enthusiastic about his job and life in general, but also enjoyed filling Steve in on his wife and family, who meant a great deal to him. Don felt he should throw into the conversation that he regularly attended a local church and that it was an important part of the family's life. He felt relieved he had worked the information into the conversation.

The course went well. There were company representatives from several surrounding states. Don could not help noticing that Steve flirted with several of the female staff, and on the last night when they had a dinner it was apparent that Steve was enjoying himself with a younger woman employee. They made little secret of heading to Steve's room before the night was over.

The next morning, they started the drive for home and Steve seemed quiet, even broody. Despite Don's best attempt to discuss the course content and how they might apply some of what they had learned, Steve was morose and sullen.

Suddenly, Steve turned to Don and said, "Look, Don, the rules are that what happens away from home stays away from home. No telling stories when we get back. I don't want to hear any gossip about last night, particularly. You get that?" he demanded with unusual aggression. Don was a bit taken back. He gave a sheepish, half-hearted response, saying he wasn't the type of person to spread stories.

There was a long silence. Just as suddenly, Steve blurted out that he wasn't to blame for his playing around. "Elaine has gone cold on our relationship. We are simply living together, sharing the same roof. I feel trapped because of the kids - they need me, but after last night and finding Jo so warm and responsive, I don't know any more."

Don felt embarrassed. "It's not my business," he muttered. He added, "We all have our problems." But Steve wanted to talk. The ice was broken. "I don't know where I am, really. I don't really know what to do or where to turn." Don stayed silent. "Our marriage has been over for years. We are living a lie. I need to do something before I am driven to despair. I am really struggling."

Don squirmed even more. He was recalling what had been said at church just a couple of weeks earlier. "Take every opportunity to share Christ as a friend when in need. Simply tell others what He does for you and why your faith is important," the pastor had said. Don's mouth felt dry.

Steve wasn't finished. "I simply don't know what to do or where to turn. I need answers. I know Elaine is under pressure, too. She really doesn't deserve a scoundrel like me."

Don took a deep breath, but just couldn't find the words to start. He turned and looked out the window.

A month later, the boss emailed a note around to the team. It read, "Steve Fergusson is on bereavement leave for two weeks. Sadly, his wife committed suicide on the weekend. The company has sent condolences."

Don was shocked and mortified. If only….

Why didn't Don take the opportunity to share his faith? The easy answer is clearly fear, embarrassment, concern about rejection, but I want to add a dimension. Most of us have been in that position at some point. Missed a chance to witness. Couldn't find the words. Even felt frustrated later thinking about what might have been. I have been, and it's likely you have been, too.

There is another angle, though. A more accurate answer to Don's problem. We are called to be Christ's witnesses and to win the lost as Jesus came to seek and to save the lost. As Jesus was sent by His Father, fully prepared for the task ahead, so we are sent out to help others to learn of Jesus. To be effective we must be prepared and be confident in the content of the message we have, which is the hope of lives. Too many of us are simply inadequately prepared and trained as well as too unmoved by the immensity of the grace we have received.

Jesus Commands

Jesus was clear to His followers: You follow Me, and I will make you fishers of men. His command to be a disciple-maker is stated in all four gospels. This is the basis on how we are to live. Each command given by Jesus in each of the gospels and the book of Acts (outlined below) emphasizes differing aspects of what a disciple is called to do:

Matthew 28:18-20
Mark 16:15-16
Luke 24:48-49
John 20:21
Acts 1:8

Matthew: Make Disciples

Matthew is all about discipleship. The heartbeat of Jesus' words in Matthew 28:16-20 is a reminder that every disciple is called to make disciples. Jesus said: "All authority on heaven and on earth has been given to me." Then He gave the church their command: "Therefore GO and make disciples of all nations." This is a command. These are the words of Jesus, given to every disciple to fulfill. When we think missions, we think "go" because many just believe missions is about going. We are commanded to make disciples as we go and wherever we go. This is the heartbeat of what Jesus told His disciples, and this is to be our heartbeat daily. The command to "make disciples" is nothing new, but is essential as believers. When we make disciples, we are to make learners of Jesus, followers who learn to follow Jesus in both conduct and doctrine.

Matthew is highlighting that fact and teaching them they have the responsibility to go and make disciples of all nations in the context of everyday life. The imperative verb in this command is to "make disciples" - this is the heartbeat of the Great Commission.

The word "go" in this commandment is not the command to go somewhere and make disciples. Many fall into the trap of thinking that missions is just about "going" somewhere. What Jesus was calling His disciples to do was this: as they go through life, teach people about Me, share the love and grace you are covered in to those who have never encountered this. Committed disciples will seek to grow in their knowledge of Jesus and seek to become, step by step, an effective disciple maker.

How do we make disciples? Jesus tells us by teaching (discipleship), encouraging, fellowship and baptism (indicating new life in Jesus). When you look at the gospel, Jesus doesn't promise a whole lot of times to be with us, but when we are making disciples, it is done in His power and for His glory. The Great Commission is embedded into the command to go. We need to remember that.

A Good Question

If the Great Commission of Matthew 28 is so important, why did Jesus leave it till the very end of His ministry? Why wasn't He on to it earlier? Why didn't He raise it and drive it home from the beginning?

There is a sense in which it took the cross and the resurrection for Jesus to be given the authority to send us out (see Psalm 8:5, Psalm 21, Ephesians 1:19, and Philippians 2:9).

New life and an ability to reproduce disciples follows from the death on the cross. Leaving it late was for a reason, and it surely wasn't because it lacks importance.

Mark: Preach to All Creation

In the book of Mark, we read the importance of preaching to all creation. Jesus told His disciples to "Go into all the world and preach the gospel to all creation. Whoever believes and is baptized will be saved, but whoever does not believe will be condemned" (Mark 16:15-16). Mark challenges his audience on the preaching of God's Word throughout the whole earth. Disciples will speak the Word—through preaching and teaching to reach the lost with the gospel.

It is our responsibility to ensure that all have heard the good news of Jesus. A disciple's purpose is to preach the gospel. A church's purpose is to preach the gospel. We must preach the gospel throughout our lives, whether that be near, far, or to the ends of the earth. Mark is clear: a disciple is called to be in the world and sharing Jesus. It is sad but true that it is unusual now for many pastors to make any sort of appeal during a sermon. No real stern challenge, no mention of eternal damnation despite its frequent mention in the Bible, no opportunity to take a public stand for Christ, eschewing embarrassment, no coverage of the imminent return of Jesus Christ for His saints. That is not the way Jesus handled His listeners as we read in Luke 12:8.

Luke: Be His Witnesses

Luke writes in his gospel and in the book of Acts that we have one role, that we are to be His witnesses, "and repentance for the forgiveness of sins will be preached in His name to all nations, beginning at Jerusalem. You are witnesses of these things. I am going to send you what My Father has promised; but stay in the city until you have been clothed with power from on high" (Luke 24:47-49).

Disciples are to preach the message of "repentance and forgiveness of sins." If you have the hope and received the gift of forgiveness through Jesus' work on the cross, then as a forgiven and redeemed person you will not want to sit still. No, you will want to tell your story of the goodness of God in your life. Luke tells us that we are to witness, to share our stories of what Jesus has done for us. Often our testimonies are not just messages on how we came to find Jesus, but how we have followed Him throughout our lives. The best story you can share is your own. Every story is unique, and everyone has a testimony of who Jesus is to them. We don't have to have had the most dramatic spiritual awakening or heard voices from on high. Just be faithful and let God do the rest.

John: Be Sent

Matthew's emphasis is on making distinctive disciples, Mark shares we must preach the gospel, Luke calls disciples to be Jesus' witness to the world, and John shares how Jesus called for us to be sent. Jesus said these words to the disciples: "Peace be with you! As the Father has sent me, I am sending you." And with that, He breathed on them and said, 'Receive the Holy Spirit. If you forgive anyone's sins, their sins are forgiven; if you do not forgive them, they are not forgiven'" (John 20:21-23). His Father sent Him into the world, so Jesus sent His disciples.

Our mission is found in Jesus' mission and He is continually looking to send us into the world. Throughout the gospel of John, we see this Jesus being obedient to His Father. Jesus said in John 5:30, "I carry out the will of the One who sent me, not my own will." Disciples are to be obedient and follow the

Father's will modeled by Jesus. "For the Son of Man came to seek and to save the lost" (Luke 19:10). The commission found in John 20:21 builds off Jesus' prayer in John 17:18. Here we see that Jesus gives the command to evangelize and shows the way to evangelize: the Father sent me, I am sending you. Our mission is modeled from the Father's sending of His Son. We are sent by the Son and empowered by the Holy Spirit. It is through the power of the Holy Spirit that we can become effective witnesses.

The Bible is clear. A review of the whole of His Word states that God has called us to serve Him in missions. He longs to empower us to be successful in sharing our faith with our family, our community, our country and the whole world. The missing ingredient is obedience. Will you obey?

REVIEW
CHAPTER REFLECTIONS

INDIVIDUALS

PRAY

1. Spend time on your knees for how you can keep God first in your life. Identify areas where He isn't first and ask for forgiveness and healing.

2. Spend time on your knees against 'me-ism,' allowing the Holy Spirit to convict and heal areas where this is prevalent in your life.

3. Spend time on your knees for submission and openness in your life, for Jesus to lead you to follow Him daily.

ENGAGE

1. What do these verses reveal about God's overall purpose and passion?
Matthew 28:18-20
Mark 16:15-16
Luke 24:48-49
John 20:21
Acts 1:8

2. God can overcome our shortcomings, but not our unavailability. What excuses have you used like Moses to say to God that you can't be an effective witness for Him?

3. What is the hardest step for you to fully be Jesus' disciple: denying yourself, picking up your cross or following Jesus? Who

can help you in your journey to grow out of your areas of weakness?

Go

1. As you go this week, who is someone you can share your faith with? Pray for specific opportunities daily to engage people with the good news you have.

2. Jonah was asked to travel to a place he didn't want to go to. There are many dangerous places you could be called to, but what promises do you know that you can rely on for safety and strength?

CHURCHES

PRAY

1. Spend time on your knees for disciples in your church to understand that the Great Commission is the call for every disciple, not just a select few. Pray for ways to make this part of the DNA and the central mission of the church.

2. Spend time on your knees praying for a disciple-making movement in your church - for others to see how they can help disciple, mentor, and coach others to grow in their daily walks.

3. Spend time on your knees for your church to be a church that aggressively and wholeheartedly wants to fish for men.

ENGAGE

1. How are you ensuring that your church isn't turning inward to the 'me-ism' in culture today?

2. Create opportunities for a culture of spiritual coaching/mentoring/discipling in your church, where older disciples can pour into younger disciples for spiritual growth and accountability.

3. What training and teaching does your church have to help develop the tools for fishing for men? How may you help develop a culture for reaching the lost?

GO

1. If you have never sent a team to visit local or global partners that your church supports, plan on making this happen in the next 6-12 months.

2. Teach your church what their role in evangelism is and provide teaching and training on how to do this successfully. Allow them to put this into action by creating opportunities for them to be engaged in evangelism - on city streets, on university campuses, or through strategic outreach events.

Chapter 3

Reintegrate

Missions is seen as an 'add-on' ministry of the church. In fact, it is the essence of the church. How do we shift it back to focus and get the balance right?

"The Lord did not tell us to build beautiful churches, but to evangelize the world."

– Oswald J. Smith

"Go, send, or disobey."

– John Piper

Having been born and raised in New Zealand for the first twenty-three years of my life, and attending church from as soon as my mum could get me in the nursery, not once did I ever hear the Great Commission preached. Not ever. Sadly, missions is being viewed by the church as an 'add-on' ministry. Let us change this and make it what it should be: missions is the emphasis of the church, an essential, integrated discipline. I remember moving to the United States from New Zealand and finding a church on almost every corner. Along a one mile stretch of road in Georgia, I counted thirteen churches. I have been in countries where there aren't even thirteen churches at all. This is a challenge.

We need to be increasing our global efforts through mobilizing, training, equipping, partnering and sending disciples globally to help people find and follow Jesus. A growing number of churches are letting their commitment to missions slide down their priority list. They have fantastic worship services, enticing and God-honoring music, uplifting worship leaders using every subtlety known, but for too many churches, it simply stops there. No mention of the Great Commission or discipling and far too few encouragements to go out and evangelize. No training, equipping or mobilizing for witnessing.

It is important to record that worship is the jewel of the church and stands unique as an activity for Christians. Long after missions have ceased, the Bride of Christ—the whole church of God—will be worshipping at the feet of our glorious Lord. Missions serve to bring people into a right relationship with God where they can worship and glorify Him. However, the pendulum has swung too far and it is time to address the imbalance. Missions and discipling have been squeezed too far out of our Christian experience. They need reintegrating into the church program and activity schedule.

A careful observation reveals that worship has become an all-dominating 'performance' in many churches, rather than a humble, self-denying act of contrition and totally God-centered adoration. It is more about me feeling good than God feeling adored. Genuine worship leads to action. Worship is the act of complete focus on the 'worth-ship' of Jesus Christ the Lord that leads to surrender, making Him Lord of our lives and responding in obedience as fully as we can. Worshipping with our voices for an hour or so a week but holding back in our daily lives is rather like Ananias and Sapphira in Acts 5 who held back something for themselves.

Micah 6:1-8 has an arresting message. Yahweh asks His people to remember what He has done for them in verse 5 – "the righteous acts of the Lord." He then questions their response by asking, "Are you going to worship Me with sacrifices, even everything you have?" The answer is surprising. He does not reject their worship, but He does say He shows man what is good and what is required of him - "to act justly and love mercy and to walk humbly with your God" (verse 8).

David understood what God wanted when he prayed, "You do not delight in sacrifice, or I would bring it: you do not take pleasure in burnt offerings. My sacrifice, O God, is a broken spirit; a broken and contrite heart you, God, will not despise." (Psalm 51:16-17). Singing and praising God alongside other Christians is so very important, but the Lord seeks something more profoundly intimate and sacrificial.

Romans 12:1-2 tells us "our spiritual act of worship is to offer our bodies as a living sacrifice, holy and pleasing to God." In other words, encountering the majesty of the Lord God, grasping something of the unsurpassing greatness of His mercy and grace, seeing the beauty of His holiness should lead to exclamations of praise in words of songs and prayer - but if that does not lead to a humble yielding of our whole selves as instruments of service everyday, then we are short-changing our God.

Scene – Balance

Pastor Alan gave himself the luxury for a few minutes to reflect on what was happening. He looked out over the sea of faces and waving arms. They seemed happy, even deliriously happy. Jono and Bev were leading the singing, backed by the growing number of instrumentalists - over thirty now. "I owe a lot to Jono," he thought. Jono's unique voice and style were attracting the young people particularly.

He laughed to himself, thinking how his elders were so opposed to the church undertaking the $10 million extensions, saying they would not fill the space. Fill it they did, and now there was a new campus across town and it was growing. Alan was sure that the bank would roll over their debt when they saw the numbers attending. They had multiple programs operating across the church for all ages and stages. It was just perfect.

Yes, it was all a pastor could ask for. Yet, something was gnawing a hole in Alan's gut. He tried to banish the thought and concentrate on Jono's music. Somehow it seemed a little hollow, almost as though it was the performance that mattered, not the words. In his prayer time, when he was close to the Lord, the thought that the church's worship time with all its focus on excellence, on a masterful production, on style over substance was somehow squeezing out the centrality of Christ. His preaching was more and more what he believed the people wanted to hear, as opposed to what they should hear. Alan was having second thoughts when he first saw the lyrics of Jono's new song, but decided not to intervene - why spoil something when it was in full flight? The words were strictly not correct, not biblical. It wasn't that, though, that frustrated him.

During the week, his in-laws had stopped in for a couple of days. Fortunately, it only happened rarely as Alan was always able to claim he was too busy to meet them. Once again his father-in-law had got at him. Alicia's father was a conservative, old time Baptist who followed the teaching of the Bible in detail. "So, Alan, when are you going to get a real missions program at your church? I see you are still running a travel service to Mexico for kids and calling it outreach. You seem to have a blind spot when it comes to the most direct and unmistakable of Jesus' commands to go and disciple." Ouch!

Alan knew he was right. He, too, had been brought up in a church committed to outreach and missions. He knew the call to be witnesses to the ends of the earth. However, he also knew that pushing this Bible truth didn't go down well with the church membership, especially the young people. He couldn't have it both ways. Alan had opted for numbers—mostly drawn from surrounding churches that didn't have the music and extras that his church offered. He tried pushing the call to obedience into the back of his mind. He could upgrade outreach sometime in the future. Suddenly, his reverie was broken by hearing, "And now, for this morning's message, here is Pastor Alan."

If we are attending the worship service, even with all of its enthusiastic and clearly genuine praise, but are not carrying that worship into our everyday lives in a sacrificial and humble manner by yielding all that we have for God's purposes, then we are in danger of the worship service simply being, at best, a happy event of limited value. Romans 6:13 suggests we need to worship God by offering ourselves to Him as those who have experienced new life in Christ, including all of our bodies - hands, arms, legs, minds - everything.

Building Blocks for Life

Deuteronomy 10:12-22 and even the next few chapters set out the principles on which we are to build our lives.

A.   "Fear the Lord your God" – fear means to reverence or worship.

B.   "Love Him" – a love that gives, not gets.

C. "Observe the Lord's commands" – Moses had hundreds of commands for his people: we have a few.

D. "Walk in all His ways" – that is every day, all the time.

E. "Serve Him with all your heart and soul" – total commitment, no 'ifs,' no 'maybes,' no excuses.

If the worship time in our church has become the sole high point, the weekly "spiritual fix," no matter how joyous and emotionally vibrant it has become, no matter how professionally and well organized it may be, no matter how close to Jesus I feel, no matter how spiritually charged I am as I leave, if there is no lasting action in love, serving, and giving, then its value is sadly limited.

Sadly, the worship time on Sunday is the only 'encounter' some are having with God for the whole week. It is enjoyable, even ecstatic, but as soon as they leave the building, the encounter is over - normal service resumes. It is one of the reasons that some people float from church to church. They are simply seeking the biggest buzz. Because it is the one and only contact with God, it is special, but it needs replicating and to be turned into a day by day, moment by moment joyfulness. Hebrews 13:15-16 says it well: "Through Jesus let us continually [that means more than just once or twice a week] offer to God a sacrifice of praise - the fruit of our lips, that confess His name. And do not forget to do good and to share with others for with such sacrifices God is pleased." Balance.

We should each be asking ourselves: Is God important enough to us to make Him Lord of all? How do we reintegrate discipling with worship in the church program? The church can help by leading us through worship to sacrifice to commitment, and by helping us by focusing on the majesty and glory of God, but it must start in our hearts. Pastors and elders should be leading such reintegration and encouraging each of us to seek a balance between worship and discipling.

Scene – In the Boss's Office

When Jack Stowers arrived at the church office there was a cryptic note for him to go to the Senior Pastor's office. Jack was the church CFO and Treasurer.

Pastor Ken welcomed him in and surprised Jack by having the elder's chairman, Charles, also in the meeting. Ken got straight into business. "We are going for a big push on numbers this year," he began. "Denny has our music and worship side really humming. He is all class and people, especially our younger set just love him and his leading. We have more people coming now, just for the music. The atmosphere is bubbly and ecstatic. We are just so glad we have Denny."

"I want to expand the main auditorium like we discussed a couple of years ago, and inside the next two years I want to plant our first suburban campus. We are thinking too small as a church, and the elders agree." Charles nodded supportively.

"What I don't want, Jack, is for you to tell me we don't have the money. I am told the extensions can be kept under $12 million and a new campus can be done on a shoestring by renting and starting small. The elders have now agreed in principle to more bank borrowing. How about you get me some updated draft budgets and we can start to figure out how to make this baby grow?"

Jack went back to his office thoughtfully. He already knew that Ken's ideas were going to put pressure on the numbers, but it would be him who had to try and make them work. He knew that the extra expenses had not translated into extra giving.

Later in the day, he had some very preliminary budgets upgraded to meet Ken's wishes. After running his eye down the columns, Ken said, "We need more than you are allowing for both projects. We will just have to make some savings and work harder on fundraising. Just remind me, Jack, why the overseas missions budget was up last year?"

Jack repeated for the umpteenth time why they were devoting more to their missions department. Jack explained the increase did not take into account any new initiatives and was a status quo budget. "Take the scalpel to the whole missions budget Jack," Ken decided. "Pick me up half a mill there. Leave the explaining to me. No one will be too worried. It's one of those out of sight, out of mind things. With a few other tweaks, we can make it all work."

The walk back to Jack's office seemed longer than ever.

Reintegrating through Planning

Some things never change. Just as eleven men were put to the test, Christ is now putting you to the test. His commissioning is as much for you as it was 2,000 years ago for Peter and his friends. Jesus is calling you with the same burden, the same vulnerable strategy, the same intense reliance on fellow humans. Are you a starter, or are you shunning the call? Are you ignoring outreach and missions? Missions and outreach is not an option for true followers of Christ. It is simply a matter of obedience. Jesus said we would be His witnesses - no 'ifs,' no 'maybes,' no excuses. We can either be a useful, influential witness or be ineffectual.

There was a court case where various witnesses were called to give evidence. The evidence was crucial to the outcome of the case. One of the witnesses was very unsure, stuttering and stammering, contradicting himself until the Judge dismissed him as being of no further value. The next witness was clear, precise and convincing. Guess which way the result went? What kind of witness for Christ are you?

Imagine what this world would be like if every disciple lived grounded in the Word, listened to the Spirit, and had a passion to make disciples through their everydayness. Imagine churches with integrated, strategic missions programs, enthusing their people to witness and disciple. What if the world around you was filled with every follower of Jesus truly living a missional life for God's Kingdom? Imagine what your neighborhood, city, community, Starbucks, schools, university campus, restaurants and office spaces would look like if every follower daily denied themselves and lived for God's glory. Imagine the conversations that could take place in the workroom, in the classroom, on the sports bleachers, between lecture halls, along hospital wards, on the lake fishing and at the office. What a different world it would be if we re-integrated missions into our daily lives and our churches raised discipling on its list of priorities.

Historically, churches relied on individuals feeling called by God to go and serve Him in various third world countries. These great men and women of faith and courage would muster up enough support to sustain themselves (mostly in very humble circumstances), and to be able to return home for furlough on rare occasions. When they did return, there would be a church meeting or meetings to allow the missionary to tell their story. Who among us hasn't sat through a 'missionary night' when we were shown faces of peoples from distant lands who meant nothing to us and we could not relate to in any way?

Many of these people did an amazing job. Some joined missions organizations that helped them achieve their calling and made the task a little easier. But somehow, it was remote from the rest of the church. There was nothing integrated or strategic about the ministry within the local church. That situation persists today in some churches with little change. There is a noticeboard in the church foyer showing photos of missionaries and threads running to countries on a worldwide map. Few stop and notice. Most barely know the people on the noticeboard and even fewer pray for them.

These churches do not have any overall missions plan, they do not manage the process: it happens haphazardly, rather than strategically woven into the church's program. We have seen young people become burdened with the needs of the unreached in some far off country, begging the church elders to bless their going, scraping up enough support and heading into the unknown. Many times, these efforts have ended in heartache, a paucity of results, a disillusioned missionary and an embarrassed church. Why? Because enthusiasm isn't enough. The church allowed itself to be pushed into a situation without taking hold of the process, making sure that the idea was part of a considered missions plan, and that the applicant was suitably trained and supported. There is no conflict between a person being called to "go" and the church taking control of the situation and managing it wisely and in a God-honoring way. How much more effective would the ministry of the faithful few be if indeed, their plans to obey the call of Jesus was integrated into a high profile missions program?

An integrated missions program would include these vital components:

1. Pastor's Initiative

It would be led from the top by the pastor. I have never known an effective missions church that didn't have an enthusiastic, totally-committed-to-missions pastor. Conversely,

I have seen churches with keen missions people struggle to get a useful missions program going in their church because their pastor just wasn't moved by Christ's commands. We have taken church pastors to Africa and Asia to see the needs and to observe firsthand what can be achieved with so little resources, and have them return and throw themselves wholeheartedly into integrating missions into their church program. The pastor must lead and be seen to be leading in order for a missions program to be effective.

2. Elders' Oversight

It would have the eldership very clearly overseeing a successfully integrated plan. Too often, churches are controlled by their pastor and his management team and the elders are rubber stamps for their ideas. The biblical model is the opposite. 1 Timothy 5:17 is clear that the affairs of the church are to be governed and directed by the elders. History is littered with failures - short and long term - of churches that ignored this approach. Funnily enough, it's the same in the corporate world. Companies with a weak board of directors disappear sooner or later. If the elders of a church take responsibility for seeing that missions, discipling and obedience to Matthew 28:19 is a high priority and is integrated into the church's culture, strategy and plans, then great things happen. Just having an elder designated to the role of missions can be a cop out. All elders need to be involved and be seen to be involved.

One of the hurdles some churches face when trying to start or upgrade their contribution to effective discipling and outreach is that the other expenses (including the pastor's and other church officers' salaries) come under scrutiny. As a result, the officers sometimes feel threatened and are reluctant to put their whole support to the program. Elders need to take responsibility in these situations and make sure that any new or better-funded program is new money, not a re-jigging of the budget.

Ultimate responsibility for the church must stay with the elders but that does not prevent the pastor leading and carrying out the elders' strategies with vigor and determination.

3. Integration into Teaching Program

Missions activities would be a woven-in part of all the church's teaching and preaching activities. This is especially needed among the young people and children. The teaching program for all ages and stages would include missions in a very obvious way. Missions would get regular mention. Missions would be accepted by the whole church as vital, exciting and effective. Training and equipping all church members in witnessing and discipling would be a regular event.

4. High Profile in Community

The church would have a high profile in the community as an active, caring, involved group. It is no good talking about it if you are not carrying it out. We must never forget about the local needs within the church and the local community. We should be readily serving and reaching out around us locally as well as globally. One of the most exciting annual outreach activities in our church (Owen) is a weekend working at a local school. We work the whole weekend tidying up, painting, re-planting, adding new facilities, renovating, etc. It's a great witness.

5. Strong Prayer Commitment

A missions-oriented church has a very specific prayer commitment for outreach and missions. While everyone should be committed to prayer for this activity, there is clearly an extra opportunity on the older members of the church who have a little more time and ability to focus on this vital need in a more formal manner.

Passion Rules

Throughout this book, we emphasize that witnessing and evangelizing is a simple, straightforward command. It doesn't need to be dressed up or explained. Jesus said, "Go." There are not too many ways to cut and dice that word. He also said, "You shall be witnesses." Not too many ways to interpret that, either. Mostly, we just need to get on with it. The biblical injunction is absolutely clear and unable to be challenged.

However, something becomes overwhelmingly obvious when you are assessing effectiveness in witnessing and missions - PASSION rules! Passion for God and passion for the lost. If there is only one message you take from this book, please take this one. This is the single most critical element to the involvement of both an individual and a church in missions: Passion reigns! Never underestimate the power of passion.

Passion arises out of obedience. It arises from drawing near to the Lord in prayer and catching something of His fierce love and vitality. It arises from begging God to give you a love for the lost around you. It arises from coming face to face with the poverty of soul and spirit, the poverty of existence, the poverty of hope in a city slum in Mumbai or Kampala. It arises from burying yourself openly and honestly in the Word of God, pleading with Him to infuse you with fervor and an intensity that held Jesus to the cross. That's where passion comes from.

If your own salvation and daily walk with Jesus is flat or lacks fervor, then obeying the commands of Jesus will be a weighty burden that will most likely get ignored. If you are finding the immensity and wonder of God's mercy a little "ho hum", then seeing a family member, a friend, or a poverty stricken Indian heading for eternal damnation won't light your wick or get you fired up to do something. If you are not too moved by the Savior giving His all on the cross in pain and anguish, bearing the punishment for your sin, then you probably won't move far to witness of His love.

We have seen people visit the most wretched and appalling of circumstances that some of the poorest of the poor live in, and come home totally won over and fired up to reaching them for Christ. Conversely, some remain unmoved. Overall, exposure to injustice, poverty and needs lights people up and shifts their passion meter. However, greater, lasting and more intense passion for the lost will come from being on your knees asking God to fill your heart with love for the needy because they sit next to you in school, in the office, on the bus, at the sports field, at the dinner table and elsewhere. If their being lost and you knowing they are in danger of God's eternal judgment doesn't stir you, then going halfway around the world to see another similar lost soul isn't likely to change you too much.

Christians and churches who have lost their passion for missions and their love for the lost ought to re-evaluate their relationship with the great merciful God, the God and Father of our Lord Jesus Christ, the Savior of the world. To know Him is to love Him, to love Him is to obey Him and to obey Him means being committed to missions. It is about having a strong Jesus connection. There is an urgent need for leadership from pastors, elders and other leaders to raise the profile of missions and the needs of the lost. For those who have a missions ministry, there is a great need, too, for reviewing your efforts. The resources available are extremely limited and need to be used well. In too many situations there is a lack of strategy, leadership, firm planning, and execution, evaluation and review.

So Much With So Little

So often we hear the comment "I do not have enough to give to make a difference." Meet Terri. She was determined to join Owen and his small team going to India to train youth leaders. She was poor, had a large family, a mortgage and a husband on a below average income. The cost of the trip was $2,000. She had savings of $500 gathered up over several years. Terri was not put off. She sold some secondhand goods, did work for neighbors, asked for support and even took a small loan.

In some of the towns visited, the temperature was 115 degrees Fahrenheit and almost 100% humidity. The Indian pastors and youth leaders crammed all of us into the rather ordinary conditions. Terri was amazing. She taught songs, how to use low cost support material, games for all ages, how to talk to teenage girls and much more.

Her contribution was overwhelming, with many of the leaders awed by her knowledge and sensitive input. Her legacy in the region is extensive, with a significant increase in young people reached for Christ.

Passion for missions alone is great, but if coupled with an eager, well organized church missions plan, it can be explosive. It will blow your socks off when you see what can be achieved.

Dear people, we can do better. We can be better stewards. We ought to be better stewards. Engaging in global missions does not mean doing our mission, it means doing the mission of God. We have the privilege of joining God on the greatest mission of this world, redemption. This is so often missed. It is time to stop seeing missions, discipling and witnessing as 'add-ons.' We need to integrate these activities seamlessly into the church program at all levels for all ages, 'normalizing' them, training for them, evaluating them and finessing the processes. It is vital that this starts at the top. When the lead pastor is involved and excited about witnessing and discipling, the whole church will be ignited.

Passion Leads to Joy

Everyone enjoys a good joke. A hearty laugh is therapeutic - even the Reader's Digest noted that laughter was medicinal. The enjoyment may be worthwhile, but it doesn't last. It's fleeting. Much of life's pleasures are like that. We get a 'kicker,' but soon it is past and forgotten. Much of what the world around us considers fun is transient and astonishingly unsatisfying. Some positive things last. I still remember with clarity and real delight leading a boy to the Lord over 50 years ago. It was the first time for me. I was elated and overflowed with joy for weeks. I could not then and do not now get over the intensity and depth of feeling that comes from the experience of leading a sinner to the Lord and seeing the Holy Spirit light up their life.

So many of us seek happiness. No one wants to be negative and misery laden. We go to great trouble to find experiences that bring us happiness, and yet often we find it's like picking up mercury with a fork - just when we think we have it captured, it's gone. Yet we will keep going back for that same experience time and time again because we know nothing else, and the need for something concrete and satisfying is close to the surface.

When we serve Christ with passion out of obedience, we lift the intensity of our positive feelings from ephemeral happiness to lasting joy. Proverbs 10:28 says "the prospect of the righteous is joy." John 15:10 states that if we "obey His commands, we will remain in His love." He added "that his joy may be in us and that this joy may be complete" (verse 11). Galatians 5:22 includes joy as a fruit of the Spirit in our lives. This is not some passing shot of good feelings, but a deep and lasting elation. Such joy comes from selfless serving.

Imagine a remote area of Nepal where there were three villages all suffering regular sickness, on-going disease, high child mortality rates, ugly, untreated sores and general poor health because there was no medical treatment of any description. Imagine finding a suitable partner who desperately wanted to build a clinic, stock it and find qualified staff for this region. Imagine resourcing him to do it and going back a year later to find the clinic completed, a nurse and a doctor working full time, and most of all, a huge measurable change in the health of the people. Imagine the 'official opening' with singing and dancing, shy mothers coming and showing you their healthy babies, old people crying with relief from weeping sores treated and gone, children freed from deficiencies. Imagine the joy, unspeakable joy, fulfilling joy. It has to be experienced to be believed. There is no parallel for this satisfaction. Such it is serving Christ and obeying Him.

The Case for Re-integration Among Short-Term Missions

In the mission world, Short-Term Mission trips (STM's) is a polarizing subject. Opinions vary across the spectrum and we have known the odd person to get quite steamed up about the subject - on both sides. A huge amount has been written on STM's - some in support, but more against or warning of the downside. In our opinion, a few STM's do a great job, most are flat out useless, and some do far more damage than good. If STM's are the only or the main focus of your church's commitment to Matthew 28, then we suggest you need to urgently re-appraise your strategy. Missions deserve a great deal more attention and input than just STM's.

Short-term trips do have the power to occasionally transform the disciple permanently, more than those they are seeking to transform. Short-term trips can help teach you who you are and who God is, how BIG God is and how insignificant you are. STM's sometimes expose us to the more outwardly evil world, teaching us how much the world desperately and continually needs to know that there is a God who loves them, who sent His only Son to die for them and through the wonderful cross they find life.

Well-prepared mission trips can mess up our puny plans in great ways that let the gospel move in us and through us. They reveal our brokenness and the need we have for a Savior. They are often the moments when God can speak into our broken hearts because we are quiet and focused enough to hear Him speak. Thrust into an alien space, out of our comfort zone, bereft of our tech toys, we are quiet long enough for God to speak. A short-term trip is not enough to be able to say, "Check! Been there, done that mission thing. It's time for someone else to do the mission thing now."

The challenge is sustaining the momentum. The very genuine heartfelt and emotional moments that occur when faced with the reality of a needy people, with great tasks begging attention, with injustice staring us full in the face are precious, but so often the passion is slowly extinguished, the commitments forgotten and normal life crowds out the Spirit's entreaty. We should never let the mission trips end. We must not change the channel and say we are glad we are not those people out there.

How to Do STM's Well

STM's, if they must be done, must start from the basis that they are done for God's glory and achieved through His power. They must be part of a church's integrated missions strategy that has specific goals and outcomes carefully planned. It isn't about us achieving some personal agenda: rather they must be designed so God can use the occasion to change those who go on them as well as those being visited. Above all, sensitivity is needed to avoid creating problems in the field. That takes experience and understanding by the planners and the leaders. Short-term trips must be developed and crafted to be the fuel for long-term engagement.

They should be undertaken with the full consent of and in collaboration with the church's existing partners. Otherwise, it's like shooting arrows into the dark with the potential for harm rather than good. If there is little respect for the partner in the field and their views are taking a back seat, then stop before damage is done.

There are many differing views on STM's. Consider these arguments:

1. If you can't share Christ at home, how come you can fly around the world to do so?

2. Intentions, even the most lofty and godly, are not enough. Planning, understanding and avoiding the dangers, and knowing what works and why are far more important.

3. Carefully consider the alternatives for spending the money before setting out. The amount spent on a mission trip put into the hands of an indigenous partner will almost always bare more fruit and create greater lasting value.

4. When sitting around in a group excitedly planning a STM, it's hard to get your mind around the damage you can do to a missionary, a missions partner, a young church, new Christians, etc.

5. The work done on STM's is often not needed, poorly done, distracting to the locals and would be better done by locals with a small portion of the money spent on the trip.

6. It often fosters a bad, paternalistic attitude.

7. It often raises expectations that end cruelly. An orphan gets a week of care and overindulgence, then gets dropped. How can a child benefit from that?

Having mentioned these potential pitfalls and criticisms against STM's, there is nothing more rewarding than seeing a young person come home totally smitten, full of Holy Spirit-infused enthusiasm and a determination to serve Christ in mission - and serve Him in an effective manner that respects the local indigenous people. STM's can be made to produce valuable outcomes.

Are STM's Worth the Risk if They are Done Properly?

Let us ask these questions: Is it worth the risk? Is it worth sending teams of people to encourage disciples, worth sending others who bring skills needed in particular areas or who can train others in skills to spread the gospel.

Is it worth the risk to you? Unashamedly, yes!

In the process, you will probably learn more about yourself and God than through most other ministries. The main risk is that the trajectory of your life may change. The risk is that you may develop a heart for that field and decide to go into missions full-time. MiT has seen this happen. You will learn about the needs of those they serve. As William Wilberforce said, "You may choose to look the other way, but you can never say you did not know."[12] The risk is that you will discover shocking injustices, abject poverty, lost souls urgently needing Christ, and want to do something about it. The risk is that you will never worship our global God in the same way again. The risk is that your prayer life will be ignited with a new passion for God's glory to be furthered. The risk is that you will help others see the needs for the Word to be spread. The risk is that your family and your church will become more missions-minded as they see your passion and drive.

Is it worth the risk for the church to send out teams? Totally, yes!

Churches are called to send out their disciples. The risk is that they will get people fired and amped up about the fields, nationals and missionaries they support. The risk is that people will come back transformed to build God's Kingdom. The risk is that they will want to see more prayer for what their church is doing globally. They will worship God in a whole new way and carry that passion into their pews, homes, groups and communities. The risk is that people will read their Bibles and pray differently for every tribe, nation, language and people group. They will call the church to better train, equip, partner, pray and send disciples globally to help people find and follow Jesus.

Is it worth the risk to God? Completely, yes!

The call of every disciple is to make disciples as they go - whether it's here, nearby, or somewhere over there. God has invited us to be part of the global solution in which over 40% of His children have yet to know about His relentless love. We are His ambassadors to go where the gospel hasn't gone before. He is always looking for more workers to send out to the harvest field. He told them, "The harvest is plentiful, but the workers are few. Ask the Lord of the harvest, therefore, to send out workers into his harvest field" (Luke 10:2).

However, the most critical question is this: Is it worth the risk to the field, the partner who will host the visit? At times, that question does not get asked at all. We think we know best and are more equipped and materially advanced, therefore the 'recipients' should be grateful and welcome our pre-determined inputs. It is so easy to get this part wrong. Be careful. Don't mix paternalism and self-centered wants with a mission partner's needs. Put the partner first and respect them and their views.

There are many mission organizations that exist to send people on short-term trips. This is a shotgun approach to missions and is potentially dangerous for the participants and for the field into which they are going. If your church must do STM's, manage them yourself in an integrated missions strategy or use an established group who has been carefully vetted and who meet very strict criteria already in your missions plan.

STM's should work with existing partners in the field who determine whether they want to engage and on what terms they will participate. This way, they know you are coming to bless and not burden them. It is important to not overstay your welcome and cause those serving on the field to be 'burdened' by a team coming. Sending short-term trips to partners that the church supports ensures accountability and follow-up for any decisions made. Clearly there is a place for well-planned and sensitive STM's as part of an integrated missions strategy.

Being sensitive to cultural issues is critical in any contact with the field. When entering a new country, a useful approach to consider is the iceberg principle. An iceberg is an amazing natural phenomenon. In one of the most beautiful and rugged parts of the

A Missionary's Account

One missionary family wrote the following to one of their supporting churches:

"We saw firsthand that First Christian Church means it when you say you are all about relationship. While financial support is critical and necessary, what every missionary needs is a supportive church family that doesn't see themselves as just a 'check writer.' We heard from you often and you asked us regularly how we were doing and how your church could encourage us in the work."

world, in the South Island of New Zealand on the glacial lake of Mount Cook, you can actually witness icebergs coming out of the water before your eyes. The principle to note is that only 10% of the iceberg is seen on the surface; 90% is beneath the surface, totally unseen. When you enter into a new country, culture or people group for a short time, you barely scratch the surface of this new environment. The surface is easy to see: you will notice certain things like food, language, dress, art, holidays. What is missing is all that lies underneath - the 90% that is not easily identified.

There are many aspects of a culture that are difficult to see and often take considerable time to grasp: history, socio-economic patterns, core values, family values, expectations, political history, concepts of justice and many more issues.

When working with those on the foreign mission field, it is important to not shift your cultural bias to where you are. It is easy to tell folks what they should be doing and how they can get it done. Culture and context are vital to understand and this is not easily attained in a short-term trip. Be sure to listen and learn, rather than insisting on expressing a certain viewpoint.

Visiting a field will give you a glimpse of what life is like in that region of the world. We must allow the field to dictate what is done and how things must proceed with their working knowledge of how the gospel will spread. The field comes first - their needs and wishes. Our job is to respect, support, care and listen. Jesus heard the heart of every individual He met. We should do the same.

Regular trips result in on-going accountability. The missionary is held to a higher standard, but more importantly, they can have regular fellowship, encouragement, love and support.

One missionary once told a church, "If you are not prepared to come and visit me, don't support me." This is a bold statement, but is a solid one. Too many churches make missions about them, their needs, what is easy for them, and place so many restrictions on what their missionaries can do that they are not effective anywhere. There are some churches that make the focus on what they want it to be - their standards, their rules, their connivances, while their partnership could be so much more fruitful for the Kingdom. Missions is not about making our lives easier, it is about partnering with God to work where the gospel hasn't penetrated. Churches need to put the interests of the missionary partner before their own interests.

When Adopting a Missionary

When a church decides to support a missionary for regular support, they become part of the church family. The church needs to establish and apply a rigorous examination of the candidate, having already determined its process for support and appointment. Understanding the conditions of the chosen field is important, so visiting with the candidate is necessary. A missionary feels that they have the support of the church when the church gets involved to that level. A missionary should also welcome visiting friends from a supporting church where practicable. Their visit is not beneficial for the supporting church only, but also for the missionary and the people they are reaching are encouraged by these visits.

Churches should not underestimate the role of prayer and the Holy Spirit's leading in setting up missionaries. When a partner is seeking support, if they don't ask for prayer first, it indicates they don't understand where the real battle lies. The apostle Paul writes to the church in Ephesus to suit up daily in the Lord, because the battle that we face is not against flesh and blood, but is against "the rulers, against the authorities, against the powers of this dark world and against the spiritual forces of evil in the heavenly realms" (Ephesians 6:12). Mission work is spiritual work, and the only way we can make any inroads is to rely on the power of the Holy Spirit in us to intervene for the battle before us.

How easily we forget that Satan is at his most active among Christians who want to do great things for God. Why would he bother with weak and aimless Christians? No need to waste his efforts there. When we take on the task of winning souls, going into all the world, evangelizing and making disciples, Satan moves into overdrive. He is going to do whatever it takes to undermine, distract, spoil or negate what you are doing through the power of the Holy Spirit. We want to push the notion of prayer for missions, missionaries, partners and the unreached. It's the one and only weapon we have. Put on the whole armor of God which includes a prayer shield according to Ephesians 6:10-20. Don't ignore it. Be slow to blame a missionary if failure happens - start with the supporting church and their lack of prayer and care.

Partnership in Practice

Where a church has an integrated missions program, all the parts are working together effectively. The church and the missionary become partners in God's work in the most profound and intimate way. There needs to be a well-considered and prayerfully written engagement document that establishes with clarity the roles and responsibilities of both parties. Both must understand and fulfill their responsibilities under such a document. Be sure to include a clear disengagement process.

Too often, the 'rules' are unclear and disagreements arise. A falling out between a church and a partner leads to a blight and a detrimental distraction not only on the church involved, but on the overall work of God in building His Kingdom. While formality is essential, it is love and grace that ultimately bind two parties together, along with an understanding that the Lord is the unseen third party to the partnership. That love and grace is the foundation for building trust and respect.

An important element in any partnership is communication. The church must keep in touch with the missionary and their work. That communication should involve all church members, not just a committee or an eldership. Focused prayer arises from a strong, regular and clear communication.

A missions-focused church has a love and passion for the lost wherever they are, and they see their missionary partner as a representative or extension of their own role. When this level of trust and respect is engendered, support becomes a more reachable goal. The prayers, love and financial support come from deep concern that is fostered by good communication.

Some churches put strict and unrealistic expectations and conditions on missionary partners receiving their support. There needs to be authentic faith with no strings attached. Many missionaries feel they can't be honest with their supporting churches, because if they were, they may lose their support. A missionary should be able to communicate with their supporters and be authentic and honest about their struggles, fears and concerns and not worry that they may be penalized because they don't have it all together. Some churches will even go so far as to say we will support with several thousands of dollars, then want to add conditions - even unrealistic conditions. No partnership can flourish if the church has ill-considered demands on its partners. Some church leaders tell their partners, "We are the experts. You have little idea what you are doing, so you need to listen to us." It's as if the partner is required to dance to a different beat in order to get the resources, prayers and support they need. Sadly, it's rare to find honest lines of communication.

Many believe that their church 'has' missionaries because they are included in the church budget as a line item. Churches don't 'have' missionaries, they send and support them. That is what the church is called to do. Sometimes the church wants a missionary to adopt a program that they have developed. They don't bother to confer with the missionary as to whether that program is feasible in their country and situation. If the missionary suggests that it will not work in their situation, the church often threatens to withdraw their support.

Churches often expect reports from missionaries to be filled with sensational stories and wonderful results. As a result, some missionaries fabricate the stories and exaggerate the statistics to please the churches. This is a very dangerous practice. Churches need to be seeking authentic partnerships in the harvest field, standing equally on a three-legged stool of love, grace and accountability from both sides to ensure a healthy and happy Kingdom partnership. The battle between heaven and hell deserves better from the Bride of Christ.

The most important message of this book for churches is that missions ought to be reintegrated into the wider program and made a priority for each and every church member.

Reintegrate
Chapter Reflections

Individuals

Pray

1. Spend time on your knees over your priorities to ensure that they are God's priorities for you.

2. Spend time on your knees for your pastors and church leadership.

3. Spend time on your knees for God to reveal to you who needs to hear the good news of the gospel. Pray for the courage and faith to overcome any of your fears so that you can be an effective witness.

Engage

1. Jesus has called us to follow Him and to make disciples. How is this playing out in your marriage, family and everyday life?

2. How do you assist others who want to go on a short-term mission trip? You can be a prayer warrior, financial giver or an encourager as they seek to proclaim the gospel to the nations.

3. What excuses have you been giving God for not being His witness and accepting the task He has given you?

Go

1. How can you be a more effective witness in your home, school, work, community and world? Who can you identify in your life right now that you need to share the gospel with?

2. Is there a desire for you to experience a short-term or long-term mission endeavor to take the gospel where it hasn't gone before? Pray for God to speak to you about how you can live out your role in obeying the Great Commission.

Churches

Pray

1. Pray for God to reveal how your church can make Him known around the world.

2. Ask God to make missions the overall mission of the church, not just a ministry.

3. Spend time on your knees for your people to have the burden for the unreached.

Engage

1. Has your church developed a global missions vision and strategy, or are they just doing things on a whim, with a shotgun approach - here, then there, then over there? How can you help your church leadership develop a solid and long-term strategy based on Matthew 28?

2. How is missions viewed in the church? Is missions seen as an "add-on" ministry of the church? If so, how could you make it the essence of the church?

3. How are you training disciples to be effective witnesses? Use your small groups ministry to help understand, study and train disciples to be effective witnesses and to gain a fuller understanding of what the Bible says on the subject.

Go

1. When was the last time you sent a team out to the field? Where did they go, and why?

2. Has the church leadership and missions team ever asked the question, "Is it worth the risk to send people around the world?" How are you helping people move beyond a short-term trip when they come home passionate for global outreach?

CHAPTER 4

RE-EVALUATE

**Time to make some changes,
starting with that very difficult word: "Sorry."**

*"The best measure of a spiritual life is not its ecstasies
but its obedience."*

– Oswald Chambers

*"We talk of the Second Coming:
half the world has never heard of the first."*

– Oswald J. Smith

Airports are fascinating places. People watching is fun - what better place than at an airport? They are places charged with emotion. They are the perfect place for witnessing tearful goodbyes and heartwarming reunions. If you are ever feeling down or gloomy, just go to the international arrivals section of your nearest airport. They are some of the happiest places on earth - you see tears not of sadness or loss, but of delight and joy.

The thing I love most about airports is you meet all types of people there. You meet the ecstatic people, those who use this time as 'social hour' to get to know you, even if you don't want to know them. This is normally when you have to overnight at an airport and you are trying to get some rest but the loudest and most 'friendly' morning person decides to sit next to you with their freshly brewed Starbucks, their fuel to keep going. You encounter the yellers who think that by speaking more loudly things will move more quickly: "I must get on this flight!" "Hurry up!" "Move out of my way!" You bump into those business people who see the airport terminal as an extension of their office, with every available power outlet occupied with their iDevices: iPhone, iPad, iPod, iMac. All the while, they make their loud conference calls landing the deal.

You meet the dawdlers who take their time at every opportunity and every line - ticketing, through security, boarding the plane, finding their seat. These are the ones who often just stop without any notice. These are the same people who drive at least twenty below the speed limit in the fast lane. They are the ones standing in line at Starbucks for more than 15 minutes, and then when they reach the cashier they don't know what to order. You know who I am talking about. Then there are the high achievers, grabbing the seats with the extra leg room, first onto the plane, carrying over the legal limit carry-ons, taking all the space in the overhead cabinets. You meet the clueless traveller in the security line who obviously assumes that taking out your laptop applies to every traveller but them, despite the numerous signs and instructions. They think their bottle of Mountain Dew will certainly be allowed through security and on board the plane.

Churches need to be like airports. A place that never seems to sleep. Busy. Open to all-comers. Processing speedily, guaranteeing safety, focused on their task. Specialists focused on their own task, but well coordinated into the team. Airports always have crowds in transit - here for a while, then heading out to their destination. What if disciples viewed themselves like planes who arrive, load up, refuel, then head out on their mission daily? We are the vessels that God wants to use in order to reach the unreached. If we don't live on mission, then sadly we become like old planes that just rust away in the desert air.

The airport arrivals hall is one of the happiest places on earth, an emotional cauldron. What if that was the emotion that disciples saw daily as they lived on mission and arrived at people's homes, work cubicles, playgrounds, schools, offices sharing the good news of the gospel with love and grace? Let us be done playing church, and let's be the church. What if we viewed ourselves as the church that can take worship experienced in the building to the streets around us? It is time to re-evaluate our purpose, our role, even who we are as God's children left here to disciple.

The Characteristics of Disciples

If we are going to make disciples, we need to know what constitutes a disciple. The word means one who learns, one who follows and one who then teaches. Discipling is by definition an on-going process for us individually, but also by generation. Young people are relying on the older generations to make them disciples so they, in turn, can make disciples of the next generation.

Discipleship is about engaging in the Word, following and obeying Jesus and going out to make disciples. An essential element in being a disciple is to be open to learning, to be teachable. It is a mindset to be continuously adopted and cultivated. For us to disciple others, we must be a better disciple ourselves. When making disciples, we are instructing others to be willing to be a discoverer. It applies to both spiritual growth as well as personal development, openness to new techniques, ideas and methods in all aspects of life. Our spiritual learning comes from delving into His Word.

Model of Discipleship

In Matthew 11:28, Jesus said we were to "take his yoke upon us and learn from him." A yoke is sometimes made out to be a device to make carrying or pulling a load incredibly easy. That is not true. A yoke halved the load, but did not remove it completely. Often a young animal - a horse, bullock or donkey - was put into the yoke with an older, experienced animal so it could learn what to do. The two who are yoked have to learn how to work as a team in complete harmony. Jesus is saying to us He will walk each mile with us halving the load so we can learn how to be effective at the work. We are not alone. We are in the best team. When making disciples, we need the courage and humility to invite those we are discipling to enter the yoke with us so we can help them with their burdens, but also teach them what we have learned. It doesn't matter where that new disciple is - at home, at work, in the community, or in some far poor country - we need to be willing to harness up with them. Whatever their need is, whatever burden they carry, get into harness alongside them and help them - disciple them.

Discipling is a lifelong process - we have never 'arrived.' Paul said to the Philippians, "not that I have already obtained all this or been made perfect but I press on to take hold of that for which Christ Jesus took hold of me. I don't consider myself to have taken hold of it … I press on toward the goal to win the prize for which God has called me heavenward in Christ Jesus" (Philippians 3:12-14). Paul was into discipling for the long haul, he was patient and encouraging just as Jesus had been with him. This is our pattern. Keep reaching up, keep battling on, don't take your eyes off the big prize and encourage those you are discipling to do the same.

Disciples and disciplers have specific goals they ought to work toward. They should be goal-oriented. I like the goal that Paul offered the Ephesian Christians in 4:11–16. He suggested they aim to work together in their various roles to build each other up, until they reached unity in the faith and in the knowledge of the Son of God and became mature, attaining to the full measure of the fullness of Christ. In other words, to become mature and Christlike. Disciples and disciplers understand and submit to the Lordship of Christ. There is a great section on this issue in Luke 14:25–33. In my Bible it is sub-titled, "The cost of being a disciple." Jesus is to be the Master and Lord of our relationships, our possessions and our very lives. "Anyone who does not carry his cross cannot be my disciple" (Luke 14:27). That's a tough call. Crosses are heavy and painful.

Discipleship is the transformation of one's heart, mind and soul for an intentional, intimate relationship with Jesus. It is about walking with Jesus daily through the stuff of life. Discipleship is a process. It is not a one-time deal or an instant arrival of where you want to be spiritually. It is not just about information, rather, it is a Jesus-centered transformation of who you are. It is a journey of discovering and resting in the knowledge of a loving God who created you and sent His one and only Son to die a sinner's death, taking the punishment for your wrongs so that by His death, burial, and resurrection, you may be made new and receive the gift of eternal life. We have been redeemed by His unending love, grace and forgiveness that was evident on the cross.

If you are a disciple, then missions is your DNA. Missions isn't optional, it's optimal in how you live with Jesus daily. It is about saying "yes" to the way Jesus called us to live. Jesus has invited us to join Him as His disciples like He did when He called His very first disciples. "As Jesus was walking beside the Sea of Galilee, He saw two brothers, Simon called Peter and his brother Andrew. They were casting a net into the lake, for they were fishermen. 'Come, follow me,' Jesus said, 'and I will send you out to fish for people.' At once they left their nets and followed Him. Going on from there, He saw two other brothers, James son of Zebedee and his brother John. They were in a boat with their father Zebedee, preparing their nets. Jesus called them, and immediately they left the boat and their father and followed him" (Matthew 4:18-22). He is still calling disciples today to change from fishing for something else to fish for men. What is it you are currently fishing for? A promotion? Love? Social status? A bigger house? Mini Cooper? Adulation among your peers?

Dragging the Chain

Too many of us are trapped in the gate lounge when there is a First Class flight to board. We have all our focus on the short term, temporal stuff when Jesus wants us to be taken up with spiritual and lasting things. We live our lives out of balance, focused on this life and with very little attention on the life to come. Paul in Philippians 3 says it rather well: Follow my example. Take note of those who live according to God's pattern. Many live as enemies of the cross of Christ. Their minds are on earthly things, but our citizenship is in heaven. We are eagerly awaiting a Savior who will transform our lowly bodies to be like His glorious body. We are not an earthly people struggling to get to heaven; we are a heavenly people walking away from earth. That is a disciple's perspective. A disciple sees the big picture, the long term and is dominated by it.

Hebrews 12:1–3 sums it up well. The writer had just done a quick summary in the previous chapter of the Old Testament guys who lived by faith, obeyed God's call, and had their priorities right. People like Abraham, who "was looking forward to the city with foundations, whose architect and builder was God" (Hebrews 11:10). In Chapter 12, we get this: "Therefore seeing we are surrounded by such a great cloud of witnesses, let us throw off everything that hinders and the sin that so easily entangles and let us run with patience the race marked out for us. Let us fix our eyes on Jesus, the author and perfector of our faith, who for the joy set before him, endured the cross, scorning its shame and sat down at the right hand of the throne of God." We can't add anything to that or try to explain it better. We just need to do it.

Jesus gives us the challenge and invitation to follow the Word, not the world, in our pursuits. Living as a disciple is an upside down way of living. It is counter-cultural. It defies reason and logic. The world says, 'I must promote myself.' The Bible says, "I have been crucified with Christ. It is no longer I who live, but Christ lives in me" (Galatians. 2:20). The world says, 'I must increase to be significant.' The Bible tells us that John the Baptist said that Jesus "must become greater, and I must become less" (John 3:30). The world tells me I will never be satisfied. The Bible tells us that we are to learn "how to be content whatever the circumstances" (Philippians 4:11). The world tells me 'I'm number one!' The Bible tells us to "humble yourselves under God's mighty hand and he may lift you up in due time" (1 Peter 5:6). The world tells me I deserve the glory for all that I do. The Bible tells us, "You are worthy, O Lord our God, to receive glory and honor and power for you created all things, and by your will they were created and have their being" (Revelation 4:11). The world tells me I need to have the latest, newest, and flashiest things to truly fit in. The Bible tells us, "Don't store up treasures on earth, where moths and vermin destroy and where thieves break in and steal" (Matthew 6:19, NLT). The world says I should and must live for myself. The Bible tells us, "Whoever wants to be my disciple must deny themselves and take up their cross and follow me" (Mark 8:34).

We are to be counter-cultural. Culturally, we need to be standing out like a sore, bandaged thumb. Not being deliberately offensive or seeking self-attraction, but in a manner that those around us will want to know why we live as we do. We need to be real, solid and reliable when everything around is plastic, shallow and fickle. In Romans 8:28, Paul writes about the transformation that takes place in us "And we know that in all things God works for the good of those who love him, who have been called according to his purpose." In God's plan everything has an ultimate purpose and through the good and the hard things we face, every disciple can rest in the knowledge that God will work all things out for the good of those who love Him. We will face trials. God doesn't exclude followers of God from not experiencing them, but He does give us the power to endure and be victorious through them. Every trial and hard lesson in life is an opportunity to learn and to grow into the likeness of Christ.

God has plans for us that He wants to work out in our lives. If only those young people who have given up on life, who distrust the institutions around them, who see so much hypocrisy and shallowness in business, in sport, in their celebrities, in their family, and even in their church could grasp what God has for them. He is the God of hope and fulfillment. Psalm 138:8 (ESV) says, "The Lord will fulfill his purpose for me: your steadfast love, O Lord, endures forever." In Lamentations 3:24-27, we read, "The Lord is my portion, says my soul therefore I will hope in him. The Lord is good to those who wait for him, to the soul who seeks him. It is good that one should wait quietly for the salvation of the Lord. It is good for a man that he bear the yoke in his youth." In Jeremiah 1:5 we read: "Before I formed you in the womb I knew you, and before you were born I consecrated you, I appointed you a prophet to the nations." We are in the safest of hands. But He is gentle, not forceful. He is caring and not constrictive. We make the choice. He waits patiently for us to respond and then when we say "yes" to serving Him, He arms and defends us, equips and blesses us. Dear people, what are we waiting for?

Discipleship is about God making us like Jesus. He wants to help us conform to the likeness of His Son. This won't happen on our own ability. We need to tap into the power of the Holy Spirit to continue to lead and guide us in our pursuit of discipleship. When we live in the power of the Holy Spirit, we are more attuned to hearing from God. He will lead, guide and show you things you would not know on your own. The Holy Spirit will equip you for the good works in spreading the gospel as He works through disciples to accomplish God's will. We need to listen to the prompting of the Holy Spirit. When we attune ourselves to Him, His voice gets louder. When we are filled with power of the Holy Spirit, we are able to live like Jesus for Jesus. He empowers us and fills us to live the way we are meant to live.

When I (Owen) got married, I thought my wife was the most beautiful woman on earth. When she walked up the aisle on our wedding day I was completely and utterly smitten, carried away by her beauty. Every fiber of my body, every emotion was totally captivated by how stunning she looked. There was no room for any other thought. The verb "be filled" is like that. When we are filled with the Spirit, we are tightly focused on one thing, with no room for any other thought or emotion. However, the Holy Spirit doesn't draw attention to Himself. Instead, He extols and focuses our attention on Jesus.

A disciple is someone who not only believes the Bible, but also will obey it. It is one thing to believe as James 2:19 points out that even the demons believe: it is a totally different story to obey the Word. A disciple seeks to embrace, follow and obey all of the Word, not just pick and choose what is convenient for them at the time. When we truly commit to following Him then we will seek to live differently, we will seek to follow Him and obey Him as we go through life. Every disciple has a role to play and that is to live the gospel and see it multiply. Jesus thought discipleship was such a big deal that He made it part of the heartbeat of the mission given to the church to "make disciples."

Churches need not only talk about the Great Commission, they need to be it, to live it, to train and mobilize their people for it. Churches need to be making disciples who make disciples who make disciples until the whole world knows. If the church truly embraces the words of Jesus, then they will arrange their staff and programs and ministries to reflect Jesus' heart to help people find and follow Jesus every day. Churches need to understand that discipleship is a process with many phases that come together over time. It is a daily pursuit and one that the church needs to equip their people to do daily.

Today many people want to see spiritual growth in their lives. They want an instant checklist to work through so they can feel like they have accomplished something. Becoming like Jesus and making disciples doesn't happen that way. It comes with intentional investment through engaging with Jesus through His Word and in prayer to His Father. A disciple is not only one who believes the Word, but follows Jesus and allows Jesus to work in them and through them. Evangelism will become part of a disciple's daily rhythm and will be the natural fruit born from one who is a true follower of Jesus, the natural result of a disciple's lifestyle. They have to be committed before they go and share their faith. Evangelism is important, but missions is about disciples living for the mission that God has given the church. Churches need to train disciples to make disciples to make disciples who are living new life through Jesus' life. We need to depend on the power and presence of Jesus.

ENGAGING IN THE WORD

Discipleship = Engaging in the Word

Being a dairy farmer in New Zealand has some very special moments. Our cows are all free range, so we get up early (4:30a.m. for me) and round the cows up from the field, walking them into the milking parlor. On still, clear days during summer and autumn, it's such a stimulating experience to see the starry sky free from the interference of city lights, then watch as the fingers of dawn slowly crawl from the eastern sky. It's inspiring. An excellent time to talk to God. A special moment to reflect on new beginnings.

There's a feeling of certainty and comfort in the rhythm of night and day. Each day starts with the same sun bursting across the horizon - there's an aura of new hopes, dreams and aspirations. Everything is fresh and new. The air is crisp. We can put yesterday behind us and start again. As someone once said, the greatest gift we have is the next 24 hours ahead of us. We begin the day with what matters most in our minds.

Think about this day. As you woke up, what first consumed your mind - work? The need for coffee? Thoughts about what you are going to wear? Whether you got your homework done? What meetings you have today? Did you get any more likes on your Facebook page? Did someone re-tweet your epic tweet? We begin each day with so many voices speaking into our lives, and it doesn't get any quieter for the rest of the day. There are many good ways to begin each day, but what is the best way? Can we challenge you to begin your day in the Word?

What if we allowed the Word to be the first voice we listen to? Often, we like to check our Facebook status, catch up on the news, check emails. Do these voices speak positively or negatively into your life? It takes a lot of effort to turn a negative into a positive, so what if we began each day with God's Word embedded into our hearts and minds? What if we dialed not into our Facebook or email accounts first, but the gospel, and allowed that to speak to our souls?

Daily we need to learn to attune our ears to His voice, His calling and His leading. We need to be in His Word as He has marvelous things He wants to reveal to us. God invites us, "Call to me and I will answer you and tell you great and unsearchable things you do not know" (Jeremiah 33:3). This happens only when we create openness in our lives by carving out deliberate time to pause and be with God. We try to fit spiritual growth into the leftovers of our lives. We are all busy. In this age of hustle and bustle, we need to get back to basics and create a simple life focused on what matters most - relationship with God and those around us.

We should be daily in the Word and in prayer. Sometimes a little bit of structure is a good way to make the deliberate step forward in our faith journey. Work out what part of the day works best for you to be open and available to meet with God in His Word and in prayer. We need to seek ways to which we can feed ourselves spiritually to keep Jesus close, as Paul says to "continue to work out your salvation with fear and trembling" (Philippians 2:12-13). To grow means to engage with Jesus through His Word. We are not to be passive spectators - no, we should be raising the bar in our own lives. The phrase "work out" means to bring something to completion, meaning each of us are responsible for our pursuit of spiritual growth and maturity through obedience to His commands.

FOLLOWING

Discipleship = Engaging in the Word + Following Jesus

Discipling was quite common in Jesus' time. Rabbis attracted followers who wanted to learn from their master, copy their life and emulate them. It was how they were schooled. Occasionally, Rabbis sought out their own pupils. They only sought the absolute best of best and insisted they follow them. However, Jesus, always the radical, sought out everybody and anybody and asked them to follow Him – businessmen, hated tax gatherers, women who were once possessed and many more. And so it is today.

A disciple will make the decision to be transformed into Christ's likeness and seek to pursue His Kingdom mission. He puts to death anything and everything that is holding him back from being all he can be in Jesus. He draws a line in the sand and says, "Yet not my will, but yours be done" (Luke 22:42). The call of a true disciple is a call to pursue holiness in all things and to change allegiance from self, the world and anything else holding them back, to Jesus and His leadership in their life.

When Jesus called the disciples to follow Him in Matthew 4, a few fishermen changed their lives from fishing for fish to fishing for men. The disciples did not know exactly what Jesus was calling them to do, yet the call He gave them was so irresistible that they dropped everything to follow Him. The first disciples obeyed without any certainty about what such a response might bring. They had little idea where the journey would lead them, and yet they followed willingly. Their ministry went from the seashore, to reaching across the oceans, to the world. Their perspective changed on what mattered the most in life as they switched to have Jesus at the center of everything they did.

Jesus said for us to follow Him. He leads, we follow. A deep, intimate relationship with God, through Christ, is the natural desire of a disciple who is genuinely saved. Our lives seek to be transformed which takes place in our hearts and affections. We grow through instruction and training. We move from not just knowing about Jesus but to personally knowing Him. We seek to understand the truth about who He is and His will for our lives. We allow Him to lead us and shape us for what we are to be and do. Jesus said to His disciples, "Whoever wants to be my disciple must deny themselves and take up their cross and follow me" (Matthew 16:24). Jesus spoke these words to the crowd and to His disciples. Jesus wasn't interested in the size of the crowd: rather, He is more interested in the size of commitment. Jesus was clear: if we really want to be His disciple, we need to deny ourselves and follow Him.

Deny Self

This is not real popular language today. We live in a world that is all about me. Me, me, me. This happens at such a young age: my toys, my food, my feelings. My, my, my.

Jesus is saying here that if you want to be His disciple, it isn't all about you. This means to acknowledge that your life is not yours. If you are a follower of Jesus, you have given your life to Him and you learn to become selfless in all things. This means a total surrender. Saying no to self and yes to Jesus. That is the standard. We don't make it about what we want, we obey what He has commanded us to obey.

Take Up the Cross

To take up your cross demonstrates the level of obedience and commitment to Jesus. A disciple lives daily in the shadow of the cross and identifies with Jesus' message. The cross was a symbol of death and torture, and Jesus is saying daily we are to die to ourselves.

Follow Me

This is walking as Jesus did, giving up control, and allowing Jesus to direct your path. It is all about obeying His will, not ours, and obeying His ways, not our ways. It is about us following then seeking to find our own followers. Giving our lives freely and completely to Him. "Be still, and know that I am God! I will be honored by every nation. I will be honored throughout the world" (Psalm 46:10, NLT). God needs to be first in our lives. We have become human doings and forgotten to be human beings. We need to be, not do, do, do. We often get ahead of God with our plans and our agenda and fail to allow Him to be God.

The best place to start is to acknowledge who we are and who He is. We are taught that God desires and wants to be known throughout the whole world, and has chosen us to be His vessels to the nations. When we are His disciples, we learn how to make disciples. We need to allow God to shape and mold us for His glory, knowing that He is faithful, true, right, trustworthy and for us. We need to train ourselves to remember that goodness and grace have been shown to us by Him. We need to declare our dependency on Him and rely on Him to strengthen us for what He has prepared for us to do. It comes back to who Jesus really is to each of us. Missions brings out people's hearts. It is a place where we are away from the noise and routine of life, and are able to allow space for the Holy Spirit to move, act and speak.

GOING

Discipleship = Engaging in the Word + Following Jesus + Going into the World

Most people, when asked to find the Great Commission, will immediately turn to Matthew 28:16-20 and point to the notion of "go" as the main emphasis in the passage. However, we believe the heartbeat of the Great Commission is to "make disciples," who then make disciples, who make disciples. Through the everydayness of life, we are called to share Jesus. Go and share Jesus today. 1 Chronicles 16:24-25 says, "Declare his glory among the nations, his marvelous deeds among all peoples. For great is the Lord and most worthy of praise; he is to be feared above all gods." This is the natural rhythm of a disciple who is daily living on mission for Jesus.

Some disciples around the world today greet one another with a greeting you don't really hear in the church today. We get accustomed to the usual exchange of pleasantries. "Hi, how are you?" followed by "the Christian F-word - Fine." Some disciples in their country, like a Pastor in India we know, will ask, "How many people did you lead to the Lord today?" If the response is none, they will go back out into the harvest field and look for more. Many lead people to the Lord each and every day, some even refuse to go to sleep until they have witnessed for the Lord.

They are committed to reaching their world for God. Toward the end of Paul's life, he wrote to the church in Rome, "It has always been my ambition to preach the gospel where Christ was not known" (Romans 15:20). Our ambition should be the same, that as we go along through life today, tomorrow, next Monday, we aim to preach the gospel and make disciples.

Next Generation of Disciples

Have you ever noticed how each older generation despairs of the next one? My grandmother was always scolding us kids for being "off the rails." My parents were sure our kids were a lost cause. And so it goes on. They have all been right, at one level. Morally, we are sliding downhill, aided by Hollywood, and post-modern culture. The Bible has this covered exceptionally well, considering it was written centuries ago. 2 Peter 3:3 says, "In the last days scoffers will come, scoffing and following their own evil desires."

However, there is also a positive way of looking at the next generation. They have buckets of confidence. I (Owen) sit with my new phone, hesitant to try anything lest I break it, lose my stuff, or do some harm. My grandson grabs it from me and fearlessly pushes the buttons until everything works. Whereas we need proof and examples of all manner of things, the millennials just dive in and do it. They are the 'do it' age group. Some of the older generations are the supporters and watchers, content for someone else to lead.

Millennials don't need leaders. They are not impressed with hierarchy or institutions. They are suspicious of corporations. Their world is smaller, waiting to be conquered. It's not so much that they question stuff, they simply ignore it, bypass it and get on. They are heavily influenced by those pushing the 'tolerance' meme. They would rather experience than be told. They yearn for authenticity and dislike hypocrisy. For them, risk beats certainty. As a group they need Christ just like everyone else. They are generally open to hearing about Jesus and represent a huge opportunity for the church. They require a sensitive, tailored strategy to be reached.

As disciples, millennials offer great hope. Their characteristics make them ideal disciplers. Once they wrap their mind around the opportunity, their energy and confidence is a veritable positive powerhouse for reaching others for Christ - both at home and overseas. It's going to take a special kind of leadership to turn their cynicism into enthusiasm, but when unleashed, this generation could conquer the world for Christ. If you're a pastor or youth leader, urgently learn the language that they listen to. Get inside their heads, reach them with skill and passion. Invest in giving them a sound doctrinal base and set them free to go and make it happen.

A Revealing Snapshot[13]

One of the most startling of international demographics relating to missions is comparing what is happening to age groups in developed and undeveloped countries. In the United States, we have an aging population and fewer young people as a percentage of the total number of people. So relatively, we have fewer young people to take responsibility for missions. In the developing world, the opposite is happening. The percentage of young people is growing dramatically in the third world. They need to hear the gospel.

Revealing Global Statistics

Country	2015		2050		2100	
	0-14 yrs	Over 80 yrs	0-14 yrs	Over 80 yrs	0-14 yrs	Over 80 yrs
USA	19.0	3.8	17.5	8.3	16.3	11.5
New Zealand	20.2	3.6	16.7	9.8	14.4	15.2
Uganda	48.1	0.4	36.0	0.5	22.3	2.9
Niger	50.5	0.2	43.9	0.3	26.5	1.5
Somalia	46.7	0.3	38.0	0.4	24.6	1.5
Nigeria	44.0	0.2	35.2	0.3	23.6	1.7

Source: United Nations Report 2015 ESA/P/WP.241.[14]

A UN report on age distribution through till 2100 shows that the ratio of older people to younger people is growing in most countries of the world but the rate is far higher in the developed world while in undeveloped countries the percentage of young people in their population increases dramatically. Birth rates are now below replacement levels in the west but in African and Central American countries the fertility rate is still more than double the developed world. For example the following table, extracted from UN reports, shows that most African countries have more than double the percentage of their population under 15 years now but this grows to nearly 2.5 times by 2050.

The ideal person to connect with a young person is another young person. The need for committed young people prepared to serve in missions has never been so critical, and it's getting worse by the day. Young people in the United States today are better equipped than earlier generations, better educated, more open to innovation and far more confident to cope with rapid change than those who are older. The church today needs to recognise that and make sure it has the right balance between worship and missions so it has an army of enthusiastic young people understanding their role in the world, willing to take hold of Christ's commands with passion and energy. Young people have the benefit of social media methods of communication. Wouldn't it be fascinating to see the hi-tech equipment we have today used for witnessing and discipling?

Sadly, what we see is church leaders catering for and indulging in a narrow experience for their young people. They are heavily into a great worship time for them, cynically copying what the non-Christian world calls music and adapting it enough to claim uniqueness and a Christian flavor. They deserve better. Christ offers them better, but too many churches are choking off the opportunity. Let's develop our focus on reaching and training millenials for Christ.

Missionaries in Training – MiT

The most important thing a church can leave the next generation is not an inheritance, but a legacy. What if churches said "yes" to making disciples at every age, and it was ingrained into the DNA of the church at every age to mobilize disciples for mission? Remember, there are no age restrictions to the Great Commission. In 2015, millennials (those born between 1981-1997) overtook baby boomers as the most populated generation in the U.S. These are the ones we should be investing in to carry the baton forward to complete the task before us. If the church fails to invest in this generation, the next generation will be at an even greater risk. Too often, young people are overlooked in their potential to make disciples.

For many young people who have a burning passion for global outreach it can be hard for them to find their way to become a missionary in their own church. To get from the pew to the field is the dream, but often the pathways to ministry are not very clear. If something stirs inside a young person and they want to find their purpose in life, what better place to do it than in their church?

A ministry Andrew developed is called MiT (Missionaries in Training). It is a strategy of global missions multiplication through intentional, relational and deliberate discipleship for fueling young people's passions for a global purpose. It is a strategy, a process, a tool and a journey for every high school and college age student to discover Jesus' call in their lives. It helps young people to see how they can use their lives for the Kingdom. This ministry is specifically developed to invest in the next generation to equip, train, disciple and mobilize them for global impact. When millennials put down their phones, disengage from culture, unplug and are open to being in church, they are looking for something real. They are looking for authenticity and transparency on how to live for Jesus. How do we impact this generation? We do it by showing them how they can truly change the world.

MiT offers young people a stepped process to truly live in a deeper way with Jesus. The gospel calls us to be something deeper than just checking in and out on a Sunday, praying the odd prayer and serving at VBS once a year. Young people crave more, and so we need to give them more. MiT is about giving young people a deliberate and intentional opportunity to live on mission with God. It is a true journey of discovery regarding who they are and what Jesus is calling them to be. This is a pursuit of a new way of living like a disciple. Some may call this radical - I call it normal.

The Apostle Paul devoted his life to mentoring and training others who were younger in the faith, like Timothy. We should follow his example (read 2 Timothy 3:10-17). Sadly, out of one hundred young people who choose to go into full-time ministry, only five people choose missions. Out of those five who pick missions only one will make it to the field full-time. Just one. Let's change the numbers. Church we must do better. It is about equipping driven, young people and harnessing their passion to find ways to knock down the walls that typically block others.

What if each of our churches had a simple and intentional process of helping people love God and love others fully through becoming a disciple of Jesus and sharing Him with others? We should encourage our young people to live a zealous life for the gospel by giving them opportunities to use their lives for something greater than themselves. The church needs to take discipleship as seriously as colleges do to train students in fields of study like medicine, law and education. When you are sick, you want to go to someone who understands anatomy, viruses and medicine, rather than leaving it up to chance. If you are in court, you would want someone who understands the law, rather than someone who has glanced in a law book and guesses what it may say. When you send your kids to school, you expect the teacher to impart wisdom and knowledge to help your children learn and develop skills in math, English and science, and not just free play. So why do churches think the training of disciples will just happen without discipline, training and equipping? The church should be the place where a disciple is mobilized, equipped and taught how to live on Jesus' mission. They will then take that knowledge and multiply themselves into someone else to make disciples who look like Jesus and live like Jesus.

MiT helps young people live daily as a disciple and become equipped to make disciples. In order to mobilize young people's lives daily with Jesus, we must get back to basics. Living for Jesus isn't meant to be complicated, though sometimes it is made that way - do this, go there, serve here, try that, eat this. MiT is about teaching a simple way for young people to live daily for Jesus through praying, reading and being.

Deeper Relationships

Any quality relationship requires healthy and regular communication. The millennial generation understands this, maybe more than anyone else. I call this generation not teenagers, but 'screenagers,' as their lives revolve around screens and social media. They use this, as they want to be loved, understood, known and valued. What if they are taught that they can have this in the fullest and deepest sense through a relationship with Jesus, and that in His Word they will find that there is One, their Father who made them, shapes them, and created them for relationship with Him? He has created them to be more than what the world is showing them to be.

To develop a strong spiritual relationship means having healthy communication with our Father. This happens through talking and listening through prayer, and allowing the Spirit to talk to us through His Word. We must help others discover the truth that when they apply the truth of the Word, the more they will become like Jesus. That is why we need to help young people cultivate the Word into the rhythms of their daily lives and to allow the Holy Spirit to speak truth into them. If you want to be led by the Spirit of God, then devote yourself to the Word of God.

In John 15 Jesus is clear about what we are to do. He explains how He is the vine, His Father is the gardener and we are the branches. We are to be connected to Him, not from anything we can do, but through all that He does for us. Our job is to:

- Abide
- Live
- Rest
- Remain

You are in the vine! But are you abiding, living, resting or remaining in the vine? The dictionary says abiding means to accept or act in accordance with a rule, decision or recommendation. The synonyms include: obey, follow, uphold, heed, accept. The key is in verses 10 to 13. It is about locking into the "branches" by being obedient. When the vital ingredients for fruit-bearing arrive from the "branches," we obey and fruit follows. If we are not connected or remaining in the vine, then we may lack fruit in our lives. Young people want to know how to abide and remain. The truth about abiding is that it comes down to this: Are you willing to believe, or willing to believe and obey? Discipleship isn't about a one-time decision. It is about devotion of our hearts and minds for Jesus.

It is all about life-on-life deep discipleship with a desire to be used for the glory of Christ.

When a disciple is obeying then fruit comes forth. So we need to ask ourselves, "Is there fruit in my life?" In order to live like Jesus and bear much fruit then we need to be with Jesus. "For from the very beginning God decided that those who came to him - and all along he knew who would - should become like his Son" (Romans 8:29, TLB). We are to become like Jesus. We do this by remaining connected in Him. So often we spend time trying to get Jesus to come where we are, rather than going where He is. We are doing our own thing. Instead, we need to follow Him and His plans.

Attraction Versus Mission

Today, many struggle with whether we are to be attractive or missional in our approach and philosophy. What if we spent less time debating which one we are and found a balance of both? We are called to make disciples, and this will look different in differing settings. We should be drawing people to the gospel through the way we live, and we should be looking for ways to share our faith.

Many churches are all about addition and not multiplication. There is a difference between adding people to the church and multiplying disciples into the world. The truth is that when we multiply, we add. We grow the church by empowering and deploying disciples for the mission that Jesus gave us to make disciples who make disciples who make disciples, which has been modeled to us since the time of Christ. When Jesus said the words, "Come, follow me," it wasn't just about getting in line behind Him - it was so much more. "Live with me, grow with me, allow me to teach you, I want to train you, I will shepherd you toward something deeper. Let's do life together and I will show you great and marvelous things, things you have never seen or experienced. Then I want you to take this knowledge and share it with others. Pour your life into them as I have done to you, and go fish for men."

Christians are becoming those who associate with Jesus, but that is the extent of it. We are becoming convenient Christians who are settling for the easy life of cruise control until heaven, or until Jesus returns. Today many churches are producing SMO's – Sunday Morning Only Christians. Much of Christianity in the American church is tailored to American standards. Jesus calls for something much deeper. He is calling disciples to make disciples, not converts. Not those who are just looking for hell insurance. We need to be leading people closer to Jesus. We can't be a disciple and follow Jesus and not obey Him. We can't say we are His disciple and ignore or disregard the Great Commission. This is the essence of who we are and how we are to live. You and I are created for so much more than what we are living for right now.

Churches need to make more than SMO's. The world needs everyday disciples who saturate the world with Jesus' love for them. Many churches think discipleship happens on a Sunday morning experience and while there are great moments on Sunday mornings through worship - breaking of bread, prayer, fellowship and the preaching of the Word - it is not enough alone, and certainly not biblical.

Discipleship needs to take place through the everydayness of accountability, spiritual disciplines, life groups and one-on-one coaching. Jesus' final words were explicit instructions on how to make disciples of all people. Jesus lived life with His disciples. He poured Himself into them. Disciples seek to do the same. It is not about 'come and see' the church, it is the church being the

Bride of Christ and declaring God's glory to all peoples. When you pour your life into someone, you feed them and nurture them to grow deeper and stronger. Disciples will look for ways to help those they coach to find deeper ways of living out Jesus' mission.

We don't just go to church. We are the church that is sent out into the world. Every disciple is Christ's messenger in a fallen and lost world. A disciple therefore, should be one who wants to help people find and follow Jesus. To find Him means they must know Him first, and to then share Him and teach others to pursue Him with all that they are. It is moving from drinking milk to eating meat. Jesus did it, the apostle Paul did it and challenged the church at Corinth to do it, so we should do it too. Move people from somewhere to someone and find their passion, purpose and life in Him.

It is time to re-evaluate where we are. Time to shift gears. And time is short. Let's do it.

All disciples are Christ-followers or Christians, but not all Christians are disciples.

Today's Christian	Biblical Disciple
- self-centered	- Christ-centered
- inward focus	- outward focus
- worship on Sundays	- worship daily
- conforming to pastor's teaching	- transformed by the Word
- comfortable	- willing to die to self
- addition	- multiplication
- church growth	- kingdom growth
- belief	- obedience

Re-evaluate
Chapter Reflections

Individuals

Pray

1. Spend time on your knees about who you can disciple right now.

2. Spend time on your knees asking, seeking and discovering how you can develop a lifestyle of living as a disciple daily.

3. Spend time on your knees asking what is your role in advancing the gospel. Are you primarily to be a prayer, giver, leader, encourager or sender?

Engage

1. Does the thought of sharing your faith scare you? If so, how can you overcome your fears or barriers about sharing the good news with others? Who can help you overcome these fears?

2. What young people can you pour into, in order to help them take the next step in their spiritual journey?

3. How are you listening to the Holy Spirit? Do you have openness in your life to hear from Him? The Holy Spirit empowers us to live on mission for Him and He has gifted and created us for specific works. If we are not careful we can miss what He has for us.

Go

1. What are you willing to give to Jesus?

2. What is holding you back from being 'all in' as a devoted disciple?

Churches

Pray

1. Spend time on your knees to cover your current missionaries in prayer, and for future missionaries to be raised up from your church to be sent into the field.

2. Spend time on your knees for a burden for the lost, that your church will see those who are "lost" not just as a category of people, but as individual men, women and children. If we fail to engage with those around us, we don't miss out on entire generations, but individuals. How can you develop a thirst for reaching individuals daily with the hope of the gospel?

3. Ask God for sacrificial giving from disciples to advance the gospel amongst the unreached.

Engage

1. How is your church making disciples and not just Christians?

2. Is your church more interested in addition or multiplication? Addition relies on a few people, while

multiplication is about engaging an entire army in the battle for the lost.

3. How is your church engaging the 6,000+ unreached people groups? How do you make this a priority for your church?

Go

1. God is a sending God. Who are the last people your church sent long-term to the field? How can you cultivate a mentality of gaining while you lose the best for the Kingdom?

2. How are you challenging your people to develop a heart to go to all nations?

Chapter 5

Renew

Revising priorities and starting afresh.

*"Give me six hours to chop down a tree
and I will spend the first four sharpening the axe."*
– Abraham Lincoln

*"You cannot reach for anything new
if your hands are full of yesterday's junk."*
– Louise Smith, Nascar driver

Effectiveness in missions is not simply a matter of having a better technique - nor is it solely dependent on us having a smart, integrated strategy, even though that is essential. The ultimate and critical ingredient is our relationship with the Lord and our willingness to love Him with all our hearts, souls, minds and strength, and to love our neighbor as ourselves (Matthew 22:37, Mark 12:30, Luke 10:27). Jesus also said, "If you love me, keep my commands" (John 14:15). The question is where to start and how to get into that space where we can be most effective at discipling. We propose that many of us, as individuals and also as a church need to go right back and start at bedrock. The Bible has some very graphic imagery for building our lives on a poor foundation. Older readers may recall singing a chorus about building a house on the sand and inviting ruin when the rain came down and the floods came up. The house built on the rock survived. Simple stuff, but full of truth. It comes from Matthew 7:24. The foundation for a fruitful, rewarding and renewed, God-honoring life dedicated to missions includes getting our relationship with the Lord on a clean, forgiven basis. David said in Psalm 51:10, "Create in me a pure heart, oh God, and renew a steadfast spirit within me." Sadly, in too many instances, we have unconfessed sin in our lives, which inhibits God from working through us. It is a major problem hindering the church, especially in missions. "If I regard iniquity in my heart, the Lord will not hear me" (Psalm 66:18).

If you have not been on your knees lately and admitted your wrongs - that you're missing the holy standard set by God's sinlessness - now would be a good time to do so. Take some time to reflect on how a holy God must abhor our trivializing sin and how easily we slip into transgressing. Think how distressing it must be for Him that having sent His Son to the shame and pain of the cross to bear the punishment for our sins that we carry on flouting the grace He offers by continuing to intentionally sin. Romans 6 helps us understand that it's possible to be a Christian but still be mastered by unconfessed sin. This can keep us from a productive life in missions. 1 John 1:9 reminds us that "if we confess our sins, he is faithful and just to forgive us our sins and cleanse us from all unrighteousness." Keep short accounts with God. Be willing to have Him wash your feet regularly with the water of the Word. The powerful imagery of John 13 is worth recounting. Firstly, it was an act of amazing humility and servanthood. In Jewish custom, the disciple always washed the Master's feet. Now Jesus is showing us the basis for serving others, "Do nothing out of selfish ambition or vain conceit. Rather, in humility value others above yourselves" (Philippians 2:3).

When Jesus washed the disciples' feet, He was illustrating the need to deal with the sin in our lives. Once we come to Christ and are saved, all sin is dealt with - past, present, and future. That is why Jesus said in John 13:10 that if a person has had a bath already (imagery for salvation), they don't need another bath - but they do need to wash their feet. Walking in sandals on hot, dusty roads in Palestine meant that sweaty feet were not in good shape for entering a home, so foot washing was common - usually done by the most menial servant. Jesus was saying that as we go through life we collect dust from the evil on the roads we travel. We need to clean our feet or identify with the sin we easily fall into, no matter how small or trivial we may think it is. These sins do not affect our salvation, but they do mar our closeness to Jesus and our ability to be effective as His servants in missions.

To "confess" means to identify with. We simply identify to the Lord that not everything we have thought, said, and done each day is pleasing to Him, and we are grateful that He has dealt with our sin at the cross. "Forgive me Lord and restore the fellowship we have so I can be more potent for You." Positionally, we are clean (saved) but practically, we need to be aware that we can ruin our closeness to Jesus and our ability to be totally effective for Him if we do not identify with the day-to-day sins that inevitably occur in our lives.

Paul called it "dying to self," daily reckoning the old nature dead. "Being crucified with Christ" is an exercise in stating that on the basis of God's mercy, all those things that are holding me back from being an effective disciple and a productive discipler are dead and buried, and through God's grace and the Holy Spirit's power, I am renewed and free of those hindrances.

When Paul wrote to the church in Ephesus, he said, "You were taught, with regard to your former way of life, to put off your old self, which is being corrupted by its deceitful desires; to be made new in the attitude of your minds; and to put on the new self, created to be like God in true righteousness and holiness" (Ephesians 4:22-24). That is a highly suitable renewed state which God can use.

We live in an era when pride and ego are rampant. It is now acceptable for people to promote themselves, praise themselves, and put themselves first. Pride is considered a virtue by many, even something to strive for. On the other hand, humility is considered a weakness. We make heroes of the wrong people and idolize those who are shockingly bad examples, while they capitalize on such adulation. People demand their rights without recognising their responsibilities, and even their rights are dubious. We seek to be recognized as someone important with a view that importance has merit. Isn't that the essence of social media? "Look at me, I am important, I have a view that you should listen to, my selfie with celebrity Joe or Jane is worth seeing."

There's an unhealthy preoccupation with self-esteem, self-love, and self-glory, and it is undermining the foundations of our society. Our culture cannot cope with such pride and self-centredness. Society relies on the glue of strong relationships built on the basis of putting the needs of others ahead of our own. When too many people are focused solely on themselves, relationships begin to unravel. We see it happening in friendships, marriages, and families, as well as in the corporate and public sectors. Sadly, this preoccupation with self has wormed its way into the church. One of the fastest-growing phenomena among Christians is the emphasis on pride, self-esteem, self-image, self-fulfillment and other manifestations of selfism. Even Tyra Banks once said, "Never dull your shine for somebody else." Well, that is a great line for those wanting to push themselves forward, but it is the very opposite of what Christ wants for us. Jesus Himself "dulled His shine" for you and me. Philippians 2:7 says "He made himself nothing, taking the form of a servant … He humbled Himself." This is the Son of God, Himself being submissive. In verse 5 Paul said, "Your attitude should be the same as that of Jesus Christ." Wow! That's a show stopper. Am I like that? Are you?

This movement is fostered by social media, which allows anyone, anywhere the self-publicity that may be seen across the world. Even worse is the childish, narcissistic fad of "selfies" - self-image promotion gone way over the top. Maybe we are not as self-obsessed as some, but it is timely to stop, take stock, and be truly honest with ourselves on this issue.

Here is a great verse to ponder: "Be devoted to one another in brotherly love; give preference to one another in honor" (Romans 12:10, NASB). It means we are to excel at putting others ahead of ourselves. We are to consciously work on seeking to make other people's needs our needs. It is the practical working out Jesus' command to "love your neighbor as yourself." It simply follows the pattern laid down by Jesus, "who being in very nature God did not consider equality with God something to be grasped but made himself nothing, taking the very nature of a servant … humbled himself and became obedient to death, even death on a cross" (Philippians 2:6-8).

Most of us are struggling to get rich. Some are so preoccupied with getting a bigger house, a better car, designer labeled clothing that they have little or no time for others. Take time to ponder this: "For you know the grace of our Lord Jesus Christ, that though he was rich, yet for your sakes he became poor, so that you through his poverty might become rich" (2

Corinthians 8:9). Can you wrap your mind around that grace? The Creator of all things, the Upholder of all things, was willing to forgo absolutely anything and everything that we might have true and lasting riches. Incredible humility. Amazing grace. A perfect pattern to follow. It is time to respond positively and humbly.

Becoming a Conversationalist

Ever noticed when some people ask you how you are they don't stop to listen – they go straight on and tell you how they are? They were not actually interested in you because they are so tied up in their own interests. Our conversations don't have so many questions nowadays. We no longer ask open ended questions because they require long answers.

Try something different to improve your conversation skills and open the door to better witnessing opportunities. Here is a simple example. Don't ask "did you have a good weekend?" You may simply get a "yes" or "no." Ask "what did you guys do on the weekend?" Wait and listen to the answer. It shows respect for the other person, shows you want to build a relationship with some depth and you are on the way to having an opportunity to say something about what Jesus has done in your life.

The words to use are "what, why, how, when" not "did, are, can, will." The academics call it obtaining qualitative instead of quantitative information. Yeah, OK.

I invite you to join me. Right now I am going to get out of my chair in my little office and I am going to kneel on the floor and seek God's forgiveness for the pride that has crept into my life. I will ask Him to give me strength to bury all that self-centeredness deep and out of reach. I am going to ask Him to help me walk a road of humility and total occupation with the needs of others, putting their good ahead of mine at whatever cost.

Did you? I challenge you to do so. Do it regularly. It is like removing a load from your shoulders. It's a release from the tyranny of selfishness and a refreshing freedom to serve. One of the biggest hindrances to effective missions is pride. Missions is essentially serving others. If our focus is on ourselves, we cannot elevate the requirements of others to

> ### St. Thomas Went to India
>
> While travelling in India for Bright Hope World, I came to a village down in the southeast which had a church called St. Thomas. I assumed it was just like many other churches that had adopted a disciple's name, but to my astonishment, the story outside the church said the doubting Thomas of Jesus' day had travelled to India to spread the gospel in response to Jesus' command. The story said he was martyred there.
>
> Think how difficult it was for him to reach India in those days. Today we can fly in a modern airliner. Do we have the courage of Thomas to take the gospel to India?

the status they deserve. I cannot think of one other thing that would release a greater wave of interest and energy in missions and discipling more than rooting selfishness out of our lives and churches. This renewal alone would be massively productive.

Looking Forward

Having dealt with the past and present, we are now renewed and fit for purpose. The new, exciting freedom in Christ, unfettered by misery and corruption, focuses on obedience, trust and honoring the risen Lord. When we are renewed, we see Matthew 28 through new eyes. It begins to loom large in our life. In this passage we find the fundamentals of our commissioning, the truth we must declare, and the command to make the good news of Jesus known to every corner of the earth. The resurrection, very fresh in the disciple's minds, is the hope of every Christian. This is what defines our faith. It is recorded in each of the four gospels, and there is undisputed external evidence pointing to the fact that Jesus rose from the dead. From a practical perspective it's difficult to see how the disciples could have been so motivated, so powerful in word and deed as to set out in Acts if there had been no resurrection. Had Jesus not risen from the dead, the disciples would have been a miserable, defeated lot returning to their former lives.

Jesus is who He said He was, God's own Son and He came to make us right before His Father. In doing so, he bore all of our sins on His shoulders. He wore the wrath that you and I deserved. Romans 6:23 tells us the wages of our sin is death. That is what we are owed for the way in which we live, but Jesus came to give us a gift that is freely ours if we believe in Him - that is, eternal life. While on the cross, Jesus said those famous words, "It is finished" (John 19:30). Death has been defeated. The resurrection confirmed it. This is a great reason to celebrate. This is the hope we have and the joy we can find as we live in the shadow of the cross, motivated by the resurrection. We are free, and in Jesus, we can find true joy, peace, and contentment. The resurrection is the hope we have in this life and the life to come. Jesus declared, "I am the resurrection and the life. The one who believes in me will live, even though they die" (John 11:25).

The resurrection generally gets bad press. Right from the beginning in Matthew 28:11-15, the chief priests tried to deny the truth of the resurrection, even though they knew it was foretold. They simply rejected what they knew was true. We live in a world where truth is deemed to be subjective. Few now hold to objective truth. According to the world today, truth is whatever you want it to be. There is one who is on the opposite side of all truth. Satan is called the father of lies and is described often as a deceiver (John 8:44). He opposes objective or absolute truth. From the Garden of Eden until now he twists truth to suit his own

Gob-Smacking Promises

"I can do all things through Christ who strengthens me" (Philippians 4:13).

"We are more than conquerors through Him who loved us" (Romans 8:37).

"He gives us the victory" (1 Corinthians 15:57).

But, hang on, how does this happen? It is no good throwing these verses around but not sharing HOW it happens.

Our source of power is God in us - the Holy Spirit. If we hand over the control of our lives to Him regularly, if we draw strength and guidance from His Word every day, if we pray for cleansing and earnestly seek for His will to be our will, then His power becomes evident. It takes sacrifice and commitment.

For missions work, it is a must.

agenda and our demise. When we stand on the truth our faith will be tested. In this life we will face hardships, difficulties and persecution for the truth we stand upon. This can make our faith stronger when we stand firm on the Word of God. The devil will not stop trying to win the war for your heart, mind and soul.

Paul explains in Ephesians 6:12 that our battle is not against flesh and blood, but against a spiritual realm where the war for our souls is waged. These battles are against "rulers," "authorities," "powers of darkness," and "spiritual forces of evil in the heavenly realms." The battle is real. In order to fight the battle daily we must dress appropriately: this means putting on the full armor of God daily (Ephesians 6:10-20). When we take a stand against the devil's schemes he will not roll over and let us have the victory without a fight. He will attack us to bring us down. God's Word is our defense.

The guards took the bribe on offer by the chief priests to say the disciples took Jesus' body, thereby planting a seed of doubt as to whether Jesus actually rose from the dead. The Bible records that Jesus lived, was crucified, and resurrected from the grave. When Jesus defeated death and rose from the dead, it inspired the disciples to go and share Him wherever and however they could. If Jesus didn't really rise, do you think the apostles would have been willing to die for a lie? Jesus shaped, trained and mobilized these disciples to be disciple makers with the task to call the world to repentance and faith in Himself. Once the apostles wrapped their head around the truth of the resurrection, the only thing they could do was to proclaim this good news. There was no stopping them. They became zealous for seeing the gospel spread.

The apostles dispersed to disciple and evangelize to the ends of the earth. At that time it cost them everything, even their lives. They suffered greatly and died for their faith. Many died as martyrs, and some were crucified on account of their witness.

Jesus' resurrection caused an enormous movement of the gospel in Jerusalem, Judea, Samaria and to the rest of the world.

We are privileged to stand on the shoulders of those who have gone before us. We can gain strength for this lofty task by accessing the resurrection power that transformed the cowardly disciples. From weak, scared, seemingly unprepared individuals they became giants, a team to be reckoned with and able to achieve super-human feats as the Holy Spirit worked through them. What they had, we can have, too. Romans 8:10-11 says, "If Christ is in you, though the body is dead because of sin, yet the spirit is alive because of righteousness. But the Spirit of Him who raised Jesus from the dead dwells in you, he who raised Christ Jesus from the dead will also give life to your mortal bodies through His Spirit who dwells in you" (NASB). This is one of the great chapters of the Bible because it confirms that if we are open to God renewing us for service for Him, we can be "more than conquerors through him who loved us" (Romans 8:37). It says, "If God is for us, who can be against us?" (Romans 8:31) This is what resurrection power is all about.

When Paul wrote to the church at Ephesus, he prayed a truly magnificent prayer for them. It starts in Ephesians 1:15. He asked the Father to open their eyes to the possibilities in Christ and that they may know "His incomparably great power for us who believe. That power is like the working of his mighty strength which he exerted in Christ when He raised him from the dead." Wow! God our Father is prepared to release in you and me this turbo-boosted resurrection power so that He may be glorified and we might have the courage, strength and stamina to serve Him and withstand the evil one. I find that overwhelming. When we go into all the world preaching, teaching and discipling, we can access resurrection power. Grab it with both hands.

Strengthened for Missions

One fascinating story in the Bible concerns Peter. He was, from the beginning, a colorful character. He was a natural leader, boisterous, first to speak even before his brain was engaged sometimes, full of bravado until it came to the arrest of Jesus, the crucifixion, and the events surrounding it. Peter was the one who wanted to take on the soldiers who arrested Jesus. He unleashed his sword and sliced an ear off a servant of the High Priest but he was the one who denied Jesus when the heat was on in the High Priest's courtyard. He went out weeping, filled with guilt and doubt (Luke 22:62). Within weeks, this same beaten man was standing up preaching fearlessly and watching as some three thousand repented and were baptized. He healed a crippled man, then he boldly stood up and challenged the leadership - the rulers, the elders, and the teachers - the same people who witnessed his denial of Christ just days before. What caused the transformation? What changed this gentle giant from a doubting denialist into the most effective mission discipler?

Consider two main, transforming events. The first was the resurrection. When Peter ran into the empty tomb and found only grave clothes, he was astounded. Peter later said that we have been given a new birth into a living hope through the resurrection of Jesus Christ from the dead and into an inheritance that can never perish (1 Peter 1:3). It was his encounter with the resurrected Christ in John 21 that had such a profound influence on this man. Paul, his associate, wanted to know the power of the resurrection in his life - power to overcome temptation, power to live a victorious Christian life, power to be an effective, fearless disciple (Romans 8:11).

The other major event affecting Peter was the coming of the Holy Spirit to indwell all of Christ's disciples. Previously, the

Holy Spirit had come upon individuals for particular ministries - but now, as part of the new relationship that God wanted with His people, the Spirit was going to permanently indwell Christians. Jesus had promised the disciples He would send this Spirit, although He didn't fully explain what the Spirit would be doing.

However, after the resurrection, Jesus didn't hang back. His final words before departing were dramatic, "you will receive power when the Holy Spirit comes upon you," He told them in Acts 1:8. And so it was. Peter was soon on his feet preaching one of the most powerful sermons of all time. Many people believe that this verse does not apply to them; that somehow that power was solely related to the early church. That belief is reinforced by the unfortunate abuse of the Holy Spirit by those claiming a great deal more than they should in the name of Christ. The truth is not that we need more of the Holy Spirit, but that He should have more of us. When we yield ourselves to Christ, putting all hindrances to death, and live in the power of the resurrection, then the power of the Spirit can be released in us.

A Message of Beauty

The Bible runs powerful imagery portraying Christ as a Bridegroom and Christians, collectively, as His Bride (Ephesians 5:25). In Lifestyle Evangelism, Joe Aldrich discusses our role as a Bride - someone of beauty and attraction. He suggests that if we lived and witnessed as Christ would have us, cleansed and washed, presented radiantly without any stain, wrinkle, or blemish, then those who do not belong to Christ would be captivated by the beauty they see in us and want to change.[15] Who doesn't love a bride? A few years ago, we (Owen and

Doreen) went to a church in another city while we were on holiday. When we arrived, two things struck us. The arriving Christians were dressed very smartly, really expensive gear, greatly overdone and flaunted, even down to the children. The second thing was their faces were non-smiling - not just long faces, but really dour and grim. No one spoke to us until we got inside, and even then it was a perfunctory "hello," and nothing more. No ushers, no bright welcome. Afterward, only one person spoke to us, and they were in a hurry. Our kids were shocked. "Dad, they aren't real Christians, are they?" my daughter asked. There is nothing wrong with being well dressed after all we are meeting the King of Kings. But there is never an excuse for a church with poor manners and sour faces. Christians are both the best and the poorest testimony to the gospel. Let's make sure we are part of the 'best' team.

Many years ago, we used to sing,

> "Let the beauty of Jesus be seen in me
> All His wonderful passion and purity
> Oh, Thou Spirit divine, all my nature refine
> Till the beauty of Jesus be seen in me."[16]

When the wise King Solomon wrote his songs, he said in an amazing prefiguring of Jesus, "His mouth is sweetness itself, he is altogether lovely" (Song of Solomon 5:16). We have a Savior of beauty, making a bride of beauty who carries a message of beauty about a future of beauty. The gospel itself is described as something of beauty. The gospel is 'glad' tidings. It brings glorious light to those trapped in darkness and evil. Isaiah 52:7 (ESV) says, "How beautiful upon the mountains are the feet of Him who brings good news, who publishes peace, who brings good news of happiness, who publishes salvation, who says to

Zion, 'Your God reigns.'" In Isaiah 61:1 we read, "The Spirit of the Sovereign Lord is on me, because the Lord has anointed me to proclaim good news to the poor. He has sent me to bind up the brokenhearted, to proclaim freedom for the captives and release from darkness for the prisoners." It is one of the most beautiful things to see when a person tangled in sin, bitter and twisted by evil, comes to Christ and the shackles are broken. Their face lights up in joy. We have a most alluring and captivating message. Let's live and look like we believe it. The end game is all about the joy of being in God's presence in a beautiful place being prepared for us by Jesus. We can live in the anticipation of heaven now and let it show in our faces, our talk, and our actions.

Your Heart is Reflected in Your Prayers

Yvrose lives in Jeremie, Haiti, the poorest country in the western hemisphere. She is an amazing woman of faith who is using her life for the gospel and the Kingdom. Since the age of 21, she has opened her heart and life to caring for abandoned and vulnerable orphans in Jeremie. When Yvrose needs help, she says, "I don't look to the left or to the right, I just look up."

She knows that her true source of strength, supply, and need is not met by what is around her or in her wallet, but what is given from above, as James 1:17 teaches that "every good and perfect gift comes from above." Yvrose inspires people to get on their knees daily and rely on God for every need, as He is the provider and supplier of every need. This lady has served over 42 years of faithful service to Jesus and gives all she can for the gospel and her orphans. It is not for riches or pleasures of this life—it is all for the glory of God.

Love – That Dreadfully Misused Word

Among the many words of Jesus is an unambiguous statement: "By this everyone will know that you are my disciples, if you love one another" (John 13:35). It's hard to avoid what is being said. Jesus managed to summarize the hundreds of Old Testament commandments into just two: "Love the Lord your God with all your heart and with all your soul and with all your mind and with all your strength," and secondly, "Love your neighbor as yourself. There is no commandment greater than these" (Mark 12:30.31).

This covers both of the axes: the vertical axis to the Lord God Almighty and the horizontal axis to each other. What is missed by many is that we are commanded to love. We don't wait for a feeling to arise. We don't look to see what we can get out of the deal before we commit to it. It is not the "love chocolate" love. It is not the "I will still love you in the morning" love. It is not even the "love you mom" as junior disappears out the door. It certainly is not the warm, fuzzy love from some pleasurable experience.

When God said He wants us to love Him, He is thinking only of the way He loves us. His love is unconditional, intentional, deliberate and purposeful. This is the action of being committed totally and sacrificially to the wellbeing of others without regard for their worthiness, even unto death. That love was demonstrated by Jesus when He suffered and died for our sins. It is inherently a deliberate action aimed at the recipient's greatest wellbeing and not a feeling although feelings may arise from our loving. We can choose to love or not to love.

God loves because love is His essence. Love is who He is. John put it very simply, "God is love" (1 John 4:16). This love is found in Romans 5:10 (NASB), "For if while we were enemies we were reconciled to God by the death of His Son, much more, now that we are reconciled, shall we be saved by His life." To die for an enemy is not what humans do. That is a God type of love. Jesus died for us while we were still His enemies and while we were sinners (Romans 5:8). He loved us first (1 John 4:19). He took the initiative. We didn't.

We have the capacity to love sacrificially because we are made in His image. To love as God loved is to make a very deliberate choice to do whatever is required at whatever cost to serve someone else's highest good with all that we can, no matter who they are or how they react. That can be immensely difficult, but if we are to be His disciples, that is exactly where we must be. We must learn to cherish, nurture, forgive and forget, serve, walk many extra miles, and do whatever is required, no matter what it costs. Tough? Of course - but worth it for Christ's sake.

It is pretty obvious that we cannot do that on our own. Romans 5:5 tells us that "hope does not put us to shame, because God's love has been poured out into our hearts through the Holy Spirit, who has been given to us." It is His love that flows through us or abroad to those around us. Ephesians 5:1 suggests we need to be "imitators of God, living a life of love just as Christ loved us and gave himself as a sacrifice to God." Galatians 5:22 remind us that love is a fruit of the Spirit. As we yield to the Spirit of God in our lives and give Him control, love will become part of our fruit. Read Romans 12:9–13:14 for a practical list of ways we can work out God's love to our neighbors. We sometimes hear Christians calling for more of God's Holy Spirit, or asking His Spirit to come upon them. Friend, we do not need to do that. We don't need Him to 'come upon us' as He already indwells us. We just need to put Him in the driver's seat. Let us renew our trust in Jesus and yield ourselves to Him so He can use us to further His Kingdom.

Prayer – The Electricity Cord

Missions begin with prayer. If we have a genuine concern for lost people, our first action should be in prayer. There are lost people all around us, at home, in our community and many more around the world - our concern for them should drive us to our knees. Jesus taught the disciples the importance of prayer in relation to missions. When Jesus was in cities and villages, the weight of the lostness of sinners pressed heavily on Him. He saw the need and He had compassion on the crowds. He told His disciples to pray for the Lord to send out workers, for "the harvest is plentiful but the workers are few. Ask the Lord of the harvest, therefore, to send out workers into His harvest field" (Matthew 9:37-38).

When Jesus said these words, the population would have seemed too large to reach for those of little faith. Today, the population is ever so much greater. Today, the harvest is still plentiful and the workers are sadly too few. The Lord frequently taught His disciples the importance and methodology of prayer. Here, He gives us one request - pray for more workers. The harvest is plentiful in China, Kenya, New Zealand, Nepal, Pakistan, and Spain - all over the world.

Here are some amazing statistics about our world: "A tremendous change occurred with the industrial revolution: whereas it had taken all of human history until around 1800 for world population to reach one billion, the second billion was achieved in only 130 years (1930), the third billion in less than 30 years (1959), the fourth billion in 15 years (1974), and the fifth billion in only 13 years (1987). During the 20th century alone, the population in the world has grown from 1.65 billion to 6 billion. In 1970, there were roughly half as many people in the world as there are now."[17]

May we be devoted to prayer so that one day together with one voice we will proclaim, "Hallelujah, Jesus is Lord!" We long for the day that will come when every tribe, tongue and nation will sing that praise. Every disciple-making movement started with a prayer movement. Before the unreached are reached, it must be preceded by prayer. Our first need is to pray. Pray to God and trust in His power and might over global issues. Sadly, today we don't really put much effort into praying for the world around us. We would like to think we do, and on occasions of major tragedy we might do so. Our hearts should be broken by the things that break God's heart.

Prayer is the fuel of global outreach. God said in Isaiah 56:7, "for my house will be called a house of prayer for all nations." Let's make it that! Let's allow the church to be a house of prayer not only locally, but globally as well. "First of all, then, I urge that entreaties and prayers, petitions and thanksgivings, be made on behalf of all men, for kings and all who are in authority" (1 Timothy 2:1-2, NASB).

The Great Commission reminds us that as we go to make disciples, we go in Jesus' authority, in His name, and for His glory. Prayer must be the foundation on which all missional endeavors are grounded and bathed. Jesus is still calling for His disciples to pray for workers to go to the harvest. Why hasn't every tribe, nation, city, people group and language heard of the name of Jesus? Is it a result of a lack of prayer? We must get zealous and deliberate in our prayers for the nations. The nations are not going to be reached because we think it's a good idea, they are going to be reached when disciples get down on their knees and pray for more workers to go to the harvest field and reach the lost with the only hope there is. Jesus has invited us to pray to Him. "And I will do whatever you ask in my name, so that the Father may be glorified in the Son" (John 14:13). We have that privilege. We must get busy praying.

The Importance of Prayer

Niranjan Adhikary is a faithful servant serving Christ in his homeland of Nepal. His ministry impact is huge. He has planted over one hundred churches in the last ten years.

On a bus ride up through the winding and narrow hills to visit Nagarkot just outside of Kathmandu we talked partnership at great length. I (Andrew) asked Niranjan what he needed most from our partnership and his answer was prayer. In the West when we talk partnership we often think of money as the means to create partnership as it is an exchange of what we have to better or help others in their situation.

Many folks want partnership to go off and be full-time missionaries, but it truly takes a special breed to be one. They will come and ask for support and almost demand to be fully funded to launch their endeavors to go. Many fail to grasp the notion and the role of prayer. Talking with Niranjan he will always ask for prayer above anything else. He knows he is utterly dependent on prayer – our prayer.

Yes, it's easy to come up with excuses for why we aren't praying:

"I don't know how" – In Romans 8, we read "the Spirit helps us in our weakness. We do not know what we ought to pray for, but the Spirit Himself intercedes for us through wordless groans. And he who searches our hearts knows the mind of the Spirit, because the Spirit intercedes for God's people in accordance with the will of God" (Romans 8:26-27). When we don't have the words to express ourselves, the Holy Spirit prays for us. He is with us through thick and thin. The Spirit understands our groans and intercedes for us. For a simple pattern provided by Jesus Himself, see Luke 11:1-4.

"I don't have time" – If Jesus took time to pray, how much more important is it for us to do so? "Jesus Himself would often slip away to the wilderness and pray" (Luke 5:16, NASB). Do I hear you say you don't have time to eat? Time for watching TV? Time for being on your iPhone, iPad? Time for golf? Time for shopping? It is simply a matter of priority. We have time for what we want.

"I don't know why I should pray" – Jesus said, "When you pray..." (Matthew 6:5). You may not be called to go, but you are called to pray. A disciple is one who prays. Even though God already knows all things, we still need to pray and beseech Him to act. It draws us closer to Him.

"I don't see any answers" – Every prayer is answered. The answer may be "no," it may be "not yet," or "yes, but because I can see the end from the beginning, not as you desire." As we grow more like Christ and use His word to understand the desires of His heart, our requests start to merge with His will.

Prayer links us to and activates the power of God. God always responds to the prayers of His people. When prayer and reading God's Word are carried out together, our prayers become aligned with what God seeks. When we are told to pray, we are told to pray in the Spirit. That means we pray in a way

One Missionary Wrote:

"The support and encouragement that we have received at the right times have given us the strength to be in this environment. Aside from the very practical support and funds – the letters, the emails and the prayers have been what's given us the big boost. Knowing that we have a group of people behind us, to vent, to talk to, to learn from and to pray with has let us know that while we're a very small number here, we're part of a larger team and working as the body of Christ as we impact this world for Him together."

that is consistent with the Spirit of God, and therefore the will of God. So prayer not only has God acting for us, but prayer is to align us with the will and purposes of God. When we pray in accord with God's will, we are lining up with His purposes.

The battle for heaven and hell is real. We live these days with every day crammed to the top, no margin, and little time left to focus on what matters most. We often try to put our spiritual growth and prayer lives into any leftover time we can find in a day. What if every disciple decided to do something new, like arranging their days around their prayer life? What if prayer was the first thing to get scheduled each day? What if every appointment, meeting, and interaction we had with others began and ended with prayer? We can fail to pray because we forget the power that is in our prayers. Without prayer, our plans and purpose will not be all that they can be. We forget that God has invited us to pray and He wants to hear our hearts.

It concerns me that I often find my praying falling into a routine where my mind is focused on a list of items I like to include. Following the pattern in Matthew 6:9-13 is obviously a good way to go in one respect, but we need to take care that we are not robots, simply parroting off our regular checklist. Routine in prayer is important, regularity is vital, but urgency and heartfelt passion is better. Have you ever prayed with such fervency and emotional eagerness that you were crying out to God?

Sometimes we need to be alone and away from everyone and all distractions where we can call out to God. Jesus did. If our burden is real for someone lost in sin, someone grieving, hurt, or in a very bad space, and it is weighing heavily on our hearts we should take the time to wrestle with God in prayer. I am always intrigued about the Genesis 32:22 story of Jacob wrestling with God. What did happen on that night?

Care

May our praying lead to caring for those we are seeking to save. The best form of service is that done in love with dignity. People matter. The Maori, the indigenous people of New Zealand, have a lot to teach the church about what matters most. There is a wonderful Maori proverb that goes like this:

He aha te mea nui o te ao (What is the most important thing in the world?) He tangata, he tangata, he tangata; (It is the people, it is the people, it is the people)

People matter. Every man, woman, and child is made in the image of God. Imagine if we remembered that each time we met someone. Imagine if they knew that. This is the gift we can share with those around us.

We are encouraged to love strangers, not just those who are like us, talk like us, think like us, dress like us; no, we need to go and show love to all. Jesus didn't come just for a certain class, social status, or race - He came for the human race. God's love is relentless and limitless. It never gives up and is full of grace - but does that characterize the love people see when they see you, a follower of Jesus? Mother Teresa said, "I have found the paradox that if I love until it hurts, then there is no hurt, but only more love."

Chances are if you are in a first world country and living in the west, you can find a caring church somewhere in your city, while in most other places - where most of the world lives - that is not the case. The world lacks compassion and grace. Caring for others is a rarity. That is how Christians can make a very clearly identified difference in the third world – simply showing love and care irrespective of the condition of those cared for.

Caring for our missionaries is vital. It means walking alongside them, sitting with the missionaries in their home, not to just check in on them, but to support, encourage, and refuel them for the work they are doing. Relationships matter between the church and the field. One missionary wrote, "Perhaps the most encouragement to us, and we mean this from our hearts, is that you actually came and visited us. You sacrificed time, money and convenience to send a small group of leaders to spend a few days with our people seeing firsthand how First Christian Church is making a difference in the Muslim world. We just cannot overstate this, actually coming to the field and listening, encouraging and sharing your lives with us was helpful beyond measure."

Many missionaries are starved for community support and fellowship, at least missionaries that are on small teams and in 'hard soil' countries. The times the First Christian Church visitors had with their 'sent teams' were among the best had on the field. These visits are the spiritual fuel that the church can provide to encourage and support what is going on. Missionaries know a true partner by those who come and walk in their shoes.

Unity

We said in the introduction that we would cover some issues that would involve blunt criticism. This is one of them. So fasten your seat belt - or, if your skin is thin, head for the next chapter.

In John 17 in that wondrous prayer of Jesus, He made a challenging request of His Father and an indirect request to us. In verse 20, He asks, "that all of them (believers) may be one." Verse 22 asks that we may be as one as Jesus was one with the Father. Verse 23 says, "may they be brought to complete unity." These four verses should blow your mind. Jesus prays an intimate, high priestly prayer, and a big chunk of it is praying for our unity as His disciples. The standard? The same unity Jesus had with the Father. That is a very big call indeed. Jesus doesn't confine His prayer for the immediate disciples - "not for them alone," but for you and I who are His disciples today. We are the object of this extraordinary prayer.

In the first instance, this prayer is about us as believers at large being one in Christ, from the cross until the end of time. This is a great and profound truth, as we are baptized into one body (1 Corinthians 12:13). Charles Hodge wisely said, "The Church is everywhere represented as one. It is one body, one family, one fold, one Kingdom. It is one because it is pervaded by one Spirit. We are all baptized into one Spirit so as to become, says the apostle, one body."[18] Who can possibly understand the full extent of the oneness that exists in the Godhead so that we might know how to live? Yet it is easy to dismiss striving for unity as being just too hard, given the diversity of interpretations, beliefs, and methods employed in Christendom.

Take a look around your city, your town, or your region. What do you see? A myriad of different churches, all with their own agenda, all set in their ways, all with the perfect reason why they are right and others are wrong. But all are undermining one of the most powerful of tools we have to take to the world when we witness - or conversely, the biggest hindrance to effective discipling. Skeptics say, "You Christians can't get yourselves sorted - why should I?"

It is simply absurd to think that any one leader may overcome the deeply entrenched differences that have existed since the early Corinthian church split around Apollos and Cephas. However, there is great harm to our testimony in seeing churches started and going forward based on the ego of one leader and a band of followers who are unwilling or unable to challenge his authority. The last few decades have seen too many such church plants and situations where the pastor is happy to be taking the limelight, comfortable to be known across the region or the nation as a 'leading pastor,' but unwilling to shun adulation, unable to be seen as a unifying influence, and reluctant to share the platform or public square alongside another. It is "my church" with "my brand," rather than Christ's church where I am a servant, seeking to bring the local body of Christ together and give glory only to Christ.

There is so much more we can do at home, on the mission field, and among churches to present a more united front, demonstrating Christ's love and compassion ahead of our doctrinal differences. We can do more to emphasize what we have in common, rather than our points of disagreement. It may take a dose of old-fashioned humility. 1 Peter 3:8 says, "live in harmony...be compassionate and humble." Simple things like being seen supporting one another in public or conducting local activities together is a good way of promoting unity.

"Is Christ divided?... I appeal to you … that you may be perfectly united in mind and thought … lest the cross of Christ be emptied of its power" (1 Corinthians 1:10–17). The outcome of a cross emptied of power is that fewer will be saved and discipled.

A Trusted, Loving Relationship?

One partner in Southeast Asia had only one supporting church. They sent him all the money he ever received for more than thirty years. There had been little contact. The church had a picture of him on their mission wall, though in honesty, the church didn't even know if it was him. The communication was difficult, as the only way to communicate was through handwritten letters sent by snail mail. It would take six weeks for letters to reach their intended recipients.

A new missions pastor, along with an elder, decided to travel to meet this partner to see the impact of his ministry. Some in the church questioned, "Why spend the money on airfares?" When they met the partner seemed very uneasy. One of the team members asked him, "What's the matter?" He glanced over to his wife, who raised her eyebrows and gave him the "You better speak up now" look. The missionary replied, "Have you come to cut my funding?" That was never their intention, but how was the missionary to know? The missions pastor thought to himself, "How sad that this is running through his mind. If we were going to cut support, we could have just done it back in the U.S."

As the tension subsided the team started to hear all about his Kingdom impact. They found out that this man was impacting six unreached countries with the gospel, he spoke six languages, had translated the entire Bible into a language for an unreached people group, taught in two different seminaries, and gave over 75% of his income away to fund a Bible college in a closed country. He funded many Bible teachers in the hills of the countries he visited, where he oversaw 10,000 house church members. Most Christians struggle to give away 10% of their income, yet this man only kept a little more than 10% for himself.

If the team had never cared and never gone, they would have never known his Kingdom impact. If they didn't want to continue the partnership, they could have just made the call from their church office to cut their support, like many churches do today to save money and eliminate the hassle. Imagine how sad it would've been if this team had not decided to go. Not only would they have missed out on a fruitful partnership, but many people in unreached countries would have missed out on hearing about Jesus.

Unreached Peoples

The needs in the world today are diverse, even daunting. However, there are many different missions organizations, individuals, and churches helping to fight against many of the social injustices like trafficking, orphans, poverty, lack of basic facilities, and many more. One of the most pressing situations is the plight of unreached people. They urgently need to hear the gospel.

Today there are over 6,000 unreached people groups. What is a people group? The Lausanne 1982 people group definition says: "For evangelization purposes, a people group is the largest group within which the gospel can spread as a church planting movement without encountering barriers of understanding or acceptance."[19] What makes a people group unreached is where there is no native community of Christian believers who can engage this people group with the gospel and plant churches. In this type of people group there are less than 2% of evangelical believers.

The presence of unreached people groups in our world 2,000 years after Jesus commanded us to make disciples of all nations is a form of spiritual injustice. It is criminal. We have been given our marching orders by Jesus. In all four gospels, disciples are called to go, preach, share and witness for Jesus to the uttermost ends of the earth. Why are there still so many who have not yet heard the truth of the gospel? We must focus on places

Risk Takers

There is a great verse in Ecclesiastes 11:1-2 that bids us "cast our bread upon the waters for after many days you will find it again. Give portions to seven, yes to eight". One interesting explanation is that the farmers alongside the Nile river would take some of their harvested wheat in the early spring and as the waters of the winter rains receded they would cast it on the damp banks taking a risk that there would be no late floods.

If their risk paid off they would get an early and plentiful harvest. God is looking for people who are hungry for an early harvest of souls and who will risk their reputation and their possessions for Christ.

where the unreached people groups live. God is saying to this generation and the next, "Stop talking about the Great Commission: live it out!" All the easy people groups have been reached - we need to go where the gospel isn't preached.

The majority of the world's unreached people groups (around 85%) exist between 10 degrees north and 40 degrees north latitude. This is called the 10/40 window, and includes the majority of the world's Muslims, Hindus, and Buddhists. The 10/40 window is also home to more than 8 in 10 of the world's poorest of the poor. Very few disciples are heading to these areas to proclaim the gospel. More than three billion people alive today are destined to hell because no one has shared how God loves them and sent His Son to atone for their sins. More than three billion souls don't know anyone who knows about Jesus. We must be willing to give everything away for the gospel. The sheer number of unreached and unengaged people groups is overwhelming, but not impossible. Don't allow these numbers to be so big that you ignore them. When you do, you don't just miss out on an entire people group, you miss out on entire generations. Sadly, most of the factors preventing them from hearing the good news are beyond their control. In many places, it is illegal to become a believer. The masses are uninformed. Many of these peoples are also unengaged, in the sense that there are no churches or agencies that are even trying to share the gospel with them.

Great Risks, Great Rewards

What is the greatest risk you have ever taken? Great risks often mean great rewards. For one lady, it was refusing to surrender her bus seat to a white passenger, spurring the Montgomery bus boycott and other efforts to end segregation. This risk taker was civil rights activist Rosa Parks. For one man, it began by taking one step up a mountain and later climbing to the top of the world. This man was Sir Edmund Hillary, a great Kiwi legend. For another lady it was deciding to become a nun, giving up the chance to marry and have children, and giving up all her worldly possessions and her family. She formed Missionaries of Charity, a Catholic order of nuns dedicated to helping the poor. Beginning in Calcutta, India, the charity grew to help the poor, the dying, orphans, lepers and AIDS sufferers in more than one hundred countries. This lady was Mother Teresa.

For one kid, it was to pursue his love of art. He started a company called 'Laugh-O-Grams' and the company went bankrupt before his first film could be created. However, he did not give up on his dream. Today, his films are legendary and he has worldwide popularity. He took risks and dreamed of a theme park where children could enjoy time with their families, take fun rides and be in the happiest place on earth. In 1955 this dream was fulfilled when Disneyland was opened by Walt Disney.[20]

The truth is we all take risks. Everyday we take risks - some big, some small. Life is risky. American writer Denis Waitley says, "Life is inherently risky. There is only one big risk you should avoid at all costs, and that is the risk of doing nothing." We are all called to do something and it is the same with our faith. God is looking for risk takers. Your response is governed largely by what priority you give to missions.

Priorities

When you hear the word "priority" what comes to mind? Kids, spouse, getting that promotion, buying a certain car, moving to a larger house? How would you answer the question, "What is most important to you?"

- spouse?
- children?

- work?
- sports?
- church?
- steak?
- Facebook?
- coffee?
- cell phone?
- football?

If you want a litmus test to help define your priorities, ask a couple of people who know you well, and see if they come up with what you think occupies the majority of your time, money, and resources. Write them down!

Don't move on until you have answered.

My top five priorities are:

1.

2.

3.

4.

5.

Today I have identified my top priority as:

_____

When we have a priority, we have focus. We align ourselves around that preference, and we are dedicated to it so that we spend considerable amounts of time, effort and energy on it. It gets the best of us. Driven people have focus. Focus defines what we are seeking to do, whether it be the pursuit of an achievement like climbing Mt. Kilimanjaro, competing in a marathon, winning a promotion, trying to get a college scholarship through football or learning to master a golf stroke. These goals are not bad things in themselves. There are many good things we can find to occupy our time and energy, but are they the best things we should be pursuing? Are they Kingdom-building pursuits? It is easy to remember the temporary and temporal and forget the eternal.

Saul was one of the most driven men in the Bible. His pursuit, his priority, his passion was to persecute followers of Jesus. We meet him at the end of Acts 7 when Stephen became the first Christian martyr (Acts 7:54-60). Witnesses to this stoning laid their garments at the feet of Saul, who gave his approval for these horrendous actions. Saul was driven - just driven in the wrong direction. On that day, a great persecution broke out against the church in Jerusalem, and all except the apostles were scattered throughout Judea and Samaria. Godly men buried Stephen and mourned deeply for him. But Saul began to destroy the church. Going from house to house, he dragged off both men and women and put them in prison. He wreaked havoc on the church, pursuing not only men, but also locked away as many women as he could.

Saul was transformed through meeting Jesus on the road to Damascus - a live encounter with the living Word. His life was completely transformed. The One he had been persecuting met him and changed him from Saul of Tarsus to become the apostle Paul. After meeting Jesus for the first time (AD 33-34), Paul turned into a missionary who sought to travel to the ends of the world and became a faithful servant through every trial and tribulation that came his way. Today, he is regarded as one of the greatest Christian missionaries. In Romans 1:5, Paul sums up his calling as a missionary to the church in Rome. He declares that the specific purpose of his apostleship was to call people to Christ. From Jesus, we receive both the generous gift of His life and the urgent task of passing it on to others, who receive it by entering into obedient trust in Jesus. John Stott says, "The highest of missionary motives is neither obedience to the Great Commission (important as that is), nor love for sinners who are alienated and perishing but rather zeal - burning and passionate zeal for the glory of Jesus Christ."[21] We have the urgent task of bringing people to know Christ. The Apostle Paul discovered God's plan for his life: "But even before I was born, God chose me and called me by his marvelous grace. Then it pleased him to reveal his Son to me so that I would proclaim the Good News about Jesus to the Gentiles" (Galatians 1:15-16 NLT). Paul knew that God had set him apart to proclaim the gospel to the Gentiles (non-Jews). The gospel was his life, and he poured himself out to see the name of Jesus go to the ends of the earth. He stopped at nothing to see the advancement of the gospel. Paul says, "I have done the Lord's work humbly and with many tears. I have endured the trials that came to me from the plots of the Jews" (Acts 20:19, NLT).

Paul shares his life's priority with the church in Corinth: "For what I received I passed on to you as of first importance: that Christ died for our sins according to the Scriptures, that he was buried, that he was raised on the third day according to the Scriptures" (1 Corinthians 15:3-4). Friends, this is it - our defining priority in life - the thing that deserves the very best of who we are and what we are about. This is our life's mission: sharing the message of Jesus crucified for us. This should be our heart's desire, to share the message and hope of Jesus with a dying and dark world. The goal is to make disciples.

When we become a committed disciple, our priorities change, our calling changes. Jesus was clear that the subject of His mission was people. Jesus commanded and commissioned His disciples to spread the good news of love and grace of God to everyone, every tribe, every tongue, every nation. The Great Commission is a command that Jesus didn't leave open for discussion. The Great Commission has not changed. It is our plans that need to change.

Renewing our hearts and lives is an essential step in becoming a disciple who can successfully disciple.

Renew
Chapter Reflections

Individuals

Pray

1. Spend time on your knees for more workers, for the harvest is plentiful and the workers are few. Pray for disciples to have boldness to step out and serve globally.

2. Ask God how you can specifically help mobilize disciples for mission through praying, sending or going with them.

3. Pray about how you can love more intentionally, using the example of John 13:34-35, where Jesus gives us a new way to live and a new way to love.

Engage

1. How are you doing in the areas of praying, reading and being? Where are you struggling? Where are you strong? What can you do to cultivate a stronger foundation?

2. How are you remaining in the vine? What specific steps do you need to take to make the connection stronger?

3. Jesus wants to have our hearts and our lives. If we are willing to follow Him, then we are willing and ready to be His disciple. What is the greatest challenge you face to live daily as a disciple?

Go

1. What are the biggest obstacles or challenges that you face for not going on a short-term mission trip? Pray over those struggles and situations so that you may one day get to experience being the hands and feet of Jesus cross-culturally.

2. If you have ever gone on a short-term trip, how have you ensured that the mission trip never ended? How has it changed your life?

Churches

Pray

1. Spend time on your knees for those in the next generation that they may be open to living globally full-time.

2. Intercede for your mission partners. Ask God to reveal how you can better support them through short-term trips.

3. Spend time on your knees for prayer revival in your church, so that your church can be called "a house of prayer for all nations" (Isaiah 56:7).

Engage

1. We must not put age restrictions on the Great Commission. How is your church at making, training, mobilizing and sending disciples in each generation?

2. How are you equipping and mobilizing the passion of those in the next generation for global missions?

3. How well do you understand the culture of the fields you serve? Spend time seeking to learn more about the 90%, and not just the visible 10%, so you can fully invest in the lives of your partners.

GO

1. When you send out short-term teams, what is the goal? How are you training them to be effective in the field? How do you ensure they bless and not burden the locals they encounter? Do your short-term trips have a purpose beyond the trip? Have you developed a strategy as to how you can use short-term trips to fuel long-term missions engagement in the field and in the church?

2. A healthy sending structure is to provide opportunity for both short-term trips and leadership trips to take place. Short-term trips are open to anyone in the church, but leadership trips are more selective. Why do leadership trips?

CHAPTER 6

RECONCILE

The privilege of doing God's work under divine appointment

"The pattern of the prodigal is rebellion, ruin, repentance, reconciliation, restoration."

– Edwin Lois Cole

"Sometimes things break and fall apart so better things can fall together."

– Anonymous

Some of the most amazing, heart-rending stories you will ever hear involve reconciliation in a torn family. One story involved a couple who drank heavily, abused their two daughters badly, separated and formed new families living in squalid conditions with new partners, with various children from various unions and a great deal of disharmony and anguish. The two original daughters grew up in their grandparents' home. As a result of a neighbor's testimony and obedience to share the gospel, one of them came to Christ. She later learned the message of reconciliation from 2 Corinthians 5:18. Skipping the details, she got in touch with her alcoholic, gambling, birth mother and led her to Christ. The mother pleaded forgiveness and she and her daughter eventually saw the father come to Christ and plead forgiveness on his death bed. Such is the power of the cross and the effectiveness of a ministry of reconciliation.

The fifth chapter of 2 Corinthians is an amazing passage. It has special significance for us as we think about missions and reaching others for Christ. It reads, "Now all these things are from God who reconciled us to Himself through Christ and gave us the ministry of reconciliation; namely that God was in Christ reconciling the world to Himself, not counting their trespasses against them, and He has committed to us the word of reconciliation. Therefore we are ambassadors for Christ as though God were entreating through us. We beg you on behalf of Christ, be reconciled to God. He made Him who knew no sin to be sin on our behalf, that we might become the righteousness of God in Him" (2 Corinthians 5:18-21 NASB). Impressive, eh?

In the Greek language, the word "reconciliation" means 'exchange' or 'change thoroughly.' It would have been used by money changers. The idea is that we exchange one situation for another, or for a restoration of God's favor. It is also linked to a word that means changing the judicial status from one of guilty to not guilty.'

In older versions of the Bible, the word is translated as "atonement" in Romans 5:11, although that may not be as accurate as it should be. Pity, because I quite like the word atonement. In Sunday school, we learned it as "at – one – ment." It comes from the Old Testament, and even had its own day in the Jewish calendar: such was the importance of the concept. It involved a blood sacrifice for the forgiveness of sins, and the making of 'one' between a holy God and a repentant sinner.

The death of Christ reconciled us to God by delivering us from death to life, saving us by His shed blood and resurrected life, and therefore from sin to righteousness, not counting our trespasses against us. Exchanging death for life. A changed status. A thorough and completely effective change. No longer guilty. Note that God is not reconciled to man, but that man is reconciled to God. No meeting halfway which is mostly the world's idea of reconciliation. It is entirely God's work, not ours. Man is the enemy of God. God is not the enemy of man. God is perfect and loves man, and out of His great love He has acted to reconcile man to Himself through the death and resurrection of His Son.

In 2 Corinthians 5, we see God's mission - reconciling the "world," i.e. human beings, to Himself. John 3:16 tells us why: He so loved the world (the human beings). Verse 19 says that God had a plan that involved reconciling us to His holy, righteous self by not counting our sins against us. Don't you just love that idea? Once we come to Him, repent, and are saved, He no longer counts our sins against us. In other words, there is no longer any condemnation for those who are in Christ Jesus, because we are set free by the Spirit from the law of sin and death (Romans 8:1-2). That is tremendously good news, and surely worth sharing. "For while we were enemies, we were reconciled to God through the death of His Son, much more, having been reconciled, we shall be saved by his life" (Romans 5:10, NASB). Having established that as His mission, God asks us to get on board. We who are reconciled have been given the ministry of reconciliation. God's done His bit, now He wants us to do our bit.

The Role of an Ambassador

Note He says it's a "ministry" and a "message" of reconciliation. So we are back to Matthew 28:19. God has set the scene, produced the ground rules and invites us onto His team so we can follow the lead and carry on His great work. Interesting the word "committed" in verse 19 is equivalent to a royal or divine appointment. We have the reconciling job handed on to us by a prestigious appointment, a royal charter.

Imagine getting a call from the White House or Buckingham Palace and being told the President or the Queen wants you to undertake a special role - an ambassador's posting. Are you going to let the phone ring on and on? Are you going to say, "Sorry, I'm too busy. I'm not interested. Try someone else. You've got the wrong person."

Another interesting point is that the verb "be reconciled" is passive. It's not that we have to undertake some major action to become reconciled as that would require an active verb. Instead, it means we simply accept in faith what has already been done for us. Equally, our job is to announce what has already been achieved. All that remains is for us to accept the completed work of Calvary.

Then there is this idea in verse 20 of us being ambassadors. Being an ambassador for your country is a very high honor. You are the appointed, official representative of the head of state in a foreign land. It is a dignified role carried out by carefully chosen representatives. As an ambassador, you carry someone else's message, not your own. You make no undertakings, promises, commitments or statements, except those of your ruler. When you do speak, your words have all the authority of your sending country.

The Romans used the post of ambassador widely. It was a highly respected role, so Paul and his hearers would have understood the concept well. Ambassadors are in a foreign land with a foreign culture. They don't absorb that culture. They retain the identity of their own country. Our citizenship is in heaven (Philippians 3:20). God has sent us into a foreign land - the world of the lost - to take the message of reconciliation. In Ephesians 6:20, Paul said he was an "ambassador in bonds." Such was his dedication and commitment to the gospel, he felt bound to his task. We make preaching, evangelizing and discipling to be something we do if its suits us, in our time, when it is convenient and we are not feeling embarrassed. How about we tie ourselves into the task so it becomes an all day, every day event?

The American Embassy in a foreign country is officially and legally a little piece of America. I have been to the U.S. Embassy in Wellington, New Zealand, not far from the Parliament buildings. It is guarded by U.S. soldiers from the Marine Corps. If I were a U.S. citizen and I got into trouble in New Zealand, I could go into the Embassy and have the full protection of a U.S. citizen back home. As Christ's ambassadors, we have a haven for people to come, where the world around cannot touch them. I love that verse in Colossians 3:3, which says, "Our lives are now hidden with Christ in God." It's a double strength fortress - first with Christ, then in God. Psalm 17:8 says, "Keep me as the apple of your eye and hide me in the shadow of your wings."

How Reconciliation Works

So we have this task of carrying the message of reconciliation. How does that work? A wise person once said, "If you take the text out of context you have a con." So, let's look at the preceding verses of the passage we just considered. In 2 Corinthians 5:14-15, it says, "One died for all and therefore all died. And He died for all that those who live should no longer live for themselves but for Him who died for them and was raised again." This amazing transformation that takes place when we are reconciled requires that we die with Him and rise with Him. Incredible, but it is the process that the Father required so we could be the "new creations" in verse 17.

In verse 18, Paul says, "all this is from God." Sometimes we're guilty of thinking that somehow we were good enough for salvation, or that we add something by our own goodness and holy actions. That is dangerous nonsense. God does it all. We were vile sinners, far from God. God is pristinely holy and utterly apart from sin. There is no way we could reach His standards - it truly is of God.

Getting a grasp of our unworthiness helps us appreciate His worthiness, and raises the urgency bar in reaching out with the transforming, reconciling gospel. In the book of Isaiah, God said that "our righteous acts are like filthy rags" (Isaiah 64:6). Yuck! If you don't know what "filthy rags" are, ask your grandmother - and not in nice company.

The latter part of verse 19 is there for a good purpose. It reminds us that justification is actually the basis for our reconciliation and the reconciliation we offer those around us. Justification is a legal term used when a guilty person is reckoned to be not guilty by the work of another taking the punishment. Actually, it's a whole lot better than "not guilty." It is the process by which God clothes us in His righteousness. He doesn't hold our wrongs against us. He removes them "as far as the east is from the west" (Psalm 103:12). One day, when you have nothing else to do, try travelling as far as the east is from the west. You will never get there. According to Romans 3:24, we are justified by His grace, through faith.

Owen's Lost Cow

When I was younger I owned a dairy farm. We had 300 cows, all free range so we had to go out to the pasture and bring them in for milking twice a day. It's a great life and I loved almost every moment of it.

The method of milking involved batches of cows so at the end of milking we knew if we had any missing. Because our farm was rolling hills occasionally a cow got left behind. Cows need to be milked regularly, especially in the spring as they get uncomfortable with the weight of milk. So off we would go, find the missing cow and bring her back to join the others in the milking parlor.

It always reminded us of the lost sheep and the gospel application. The 99 was not good enough for Jesus and 299 cows wasn't good enough for us. We loved all our animals and simply had to go looking for any lost.

If only I was that diligent for lost souls.

Another Bible term which adds to our understanding is in 1 John 4:10 where it says, "This is love, not that we loved God, but that he loved us and sent his son as an atoning sacrifice for our sins." It is used again in 1 John 2:2. The idea is propitiation. It means a sacrifice that is designed to appease for our sins. Throughout time various people have tried to appease God by some sort of sacrifice. One poor fellow, a monk, walked on his hands and knees for miles, smiting his head on the ground with every step forward. An unbelievable sacrifice, but nowhere near being able to appease God's wrath against our sin.

No sacrifice we can make will do it. God Himself had to supply a lamb - His only begotten, spotless, sin-apart, holy Son. He and His sacrifice could do it. That is what the cross is all about. God the Father sacrificed His son for our sins that we might be reconciled to Him in His holy state. Hebrews 9:14 reminds us that "the blood of Christ who offered himself, unblemished to God cleanses us from the acts that would have led to death."

One last thing on this great subject. Verse 20 says God is "making his appeal through us." Yes, friend, God is appealing to sinners to be saved and reconciled. His love has no limits. He so badly wants us all to come to Him. God does not desire any to perish (Matthew 18:19; 2 Peter 3:9). And notice His appeal is through us. Sinners may stop their ears and not listen, but never let it be said they didn't hear because we had our ears blocked when God wants to make that appeal through us. Remember, we are ambassadors. We are on call twenty-four hours per day. Now there's a nagging thought to sleep on tonight!

Has the wonder and the immensity of reconciliation occurred to you? Are you moved by the immensity of God's love and mercy? The great un-bridgeable gap between a holy, totally sinless God and willfully sinning man has been dealt to by the only means possible – a spotless, substitutionary sacrifice provided freely in love. Wow!! What a small price we have to pay to be part of His mission and have the ministry of reconciliation. 2 Corinthians 6:1-2 says, "As God's fellow workers we urge you not to receive the grace of God in vain. For he says - in the time of my favor I heard you and in the day of salvation I helped you. I tell you now is the time of God's favor, now is the day of salvation." Yes, God is appealing and we are urging the lost to come to Him and be reconciled. Like the Good Shepherd, we need to go hunting for the lost sheep.

The ministry of reconciliation includes forgiveness and reconciliation between people. Most people have a story in their family history of some sort of split. Maybe it was a will that was challenged, a disagreement about land or a house, a falling out among in-laws, but often such fractures involve money. My (Owen) great, great grandfather (and if you haven't worked it out, it was Andrew's great, great, great grandfather!) was a lawyer in London, England with his two brothers. In the 1840's, he did a silly thing. He lent money from the trust fund to a friend who could not pay it back. The two brothers were horrified, and banned him to the south of France. After some reflection, they decided the south of France was not far enough away, so they wrote him a letter (I have the actual letter they wrote) and demanded he appear at the port of Southampton in the south of England, heavily disguised, in case the brothers would be further shamed, so he could be dispatched by ship to Canada.

On the day appointed at the port, the ship to Canada was delayed. The brothers then gave the miscreant a choice - there were boats sailing to South Africa and to New Zealand. "Take your choice." For whatever reason - maybe the flip of a coin - my forebear chose New Zealand. That's how close I was to being Canadian or South African! Along with his wife and seven children, they sailed for Wellington, New Zealand. He later sought reconciliation with his brothers, but the correspondence shows not a whit of forgiveness. He had done his chips, caused great embarrassment, and he was not welcomed back. The mother of the brothers was different. Unbeknown to the two lawyers, she carried on writing to my forebear, and even sent him quite large sums of money and family silver. (All of that disappeared long before I arrived on the family tree!). The story is interesting for us as his descendants, but it does show how mistakes have consequences, and those consequences can lead to years of bitterness, loneliness, heartache and lost opportunity. My great, great grandfather was unhappy with his lot - a lawyer trying to be a farmer doesn't always work, and he died a rather forlorn, unsatisfied fellow. Disagreements weaken both parties, no matter how justified one side may be. They lead to resentment, frustration, hurt, and most of all unfulfilled promise, lost opportunity and a warping of the mind affecting the whole person.

Often pride is all that stands between warring parties and reconciliation. It is particularly unhelpful when Christians get involved in public spats. It damages our testimony. It is an anathema and a slight to a loving, forgiving Savior. Part of the ministry of reconciliation is to be forgiving and healing in our relationships, even when we are the offended party. If we can gently steer two disagreeing parties through the path of reconciliation, we add great value to their lives and honor the One who thought our reconciliation to God was so important, He died for it. Most of us love the parable of the "forgiving father," sometimes known as the "prodigal son." Luke, the medic and historian collected human interest stories from the life of Jesus. He would have been the sort of doctor you would not mind going to - kind, gentle and thoughtful. He recorded this great story about a loving, forgiving father (Luke 15:11-32).

At the time the big names in the religious scene were getting upset with Jesus (Luke 15:1-2). They had seen enough of His miracles and heard enough of His wise words of love and forgiveness to be intrigued - but they were offended. They lurked in the shadows, hung around the edge of the crowds to listen, but tried not to look too interested. Being so holy and righteous in their own minds, they were getting antsy with Jesus for spending too much time with the 'down and outs.' They found it incomprehensible that Jesus would hang out with these 'low lifes.' They started muttering and murmuring. It's easy to imagine them with their flowing robes and flashy bling and their stern appearance. I love it when Jesus called them out as "painted gravestones" (Matthew 23:27). That's what you call getting 'hit between the eyes.'

You can imagine what happened when Jesus got to the part of the parable that mentions the "older brother." Actually, the story was more about this conceited snob than it was about the pig feeder. The big shot Pharisees would have been fuming. They knew they were getting called out. It is very telling that we don't know what happened to the older brother in the parable. We know he had not entered the house, but such is the mercy and grace of our God that there was still time for reconciliation.

In my (Owen) childhood home, we used to have a copy of William Holman Hunt's picture, "The Light of the World" on the wall in our sitting room. The picture was a rather dark work of Christ standing at the door knocking, holding a lamp. It was based on Revelation 3:19-20, which says, "Be earnest and repent. Here am I. I stand at the door and knock. If anyone hears my voice and opens the door I will come in and eat with him and he with me." It may be that you're reading this and have never become a Christian. Maybe you have never repented and opened your heart to Jesus and acknowledged Him as your Savior and Lord. Maybe you have never enjoyed the experience of having Him come into your life, reconciling you to Himself and having Him fellowship with you.

As sincerely as I can say, I want to urge you to please take the opportunity right now. Stop your reading and take a few minutes to consider how your sin and wrongdoing is offensive to a holy God, and is stopping you from knowing Him. Think how He loved you enough to come into the world as Jesus, lived a sinless life, and went to the cross to die for you, taking the punishment for your wrong. Remind yourself that He rose from the dead that you might have life, and ask Him to come into your life, forgive you, cleanse you and be your Lord. You might simply pray these words:

> Father God, I acknowledge I am a sinner and cannot save myself no matter how hard I try. I realize this sin keeps me from You. Please forgive me as I accept that You took the penalty on the cross for all of my wrongs. I repent of my wrongdoing. I ask You to come into my life as my Savior and Lord. Help me to live as a new person in Christ. Amen.

If you genuinely pray that prayer, on the authority of the Word of God, you will certainly be saved and filled with the Holy Spirit (1 John 5:9-12). You receive God's gift of salvation by His grace when you put your faith in Christ, repent of your sin, confess Christ as your Lord and Savior and are baptized by immersion to be united into Jesus death, burial and resurrection (Romans 6). Find a Bible-believing church and tell them you have accepted Jesus as your Lord and Savior and want to be baptized. Baptism is an act of obedient faith and outward expression of an inward transformation.

To those of you who are Christians, there is a time when Christ stands at the door seeking reconciliation, seeking you to forgive and forget, to deal with some issues that are keeping you from full fellowship with Him. It is time to open the door to Him and welcome Him back. He has never gone away. You do not lose your salvation - that would belittle the all-powerful atoning work of the cross. However, it is possible that enmity, bitterness or estrangement from family or friends is damaging your witness and limiting your ability to be a disciple and disciple others.

It's time to kick pride in the guts, get back on your knees and get that door open again restoring the fellowship - that's what the eating bit refers to in Revelation 3:20. You will not believe the relief that sweeps over you if you are sincere. Prune the dead wood and become fruitful again. It is much more exciting and satisfying than nursing grudges. Then go and sit down with the one who hurt you or the person you may have hurt and make things right with them if you possibly can. It's biblical and it's therapeutic.

Full individual reconciliation is a strong basis for effective missions, locally and globally. Understanding the vital truths is a great start but adopting and practicing the "ministry of reconciliation" is much more effective. A completely cleansed life on the basis of Christ's atoning work is essential but carrying the message of reconciliation to others and living out the principles of reconciliation are highly effective mission tools.

The world is crying out for more dedicated ambassadors – representatives of a loving Father operating in a fallen, needy world.

RECONCILE
CHAPTER REFLECTIONS

INDIVIDUALS

PRAY

1. Spend time on your knees asking God to make you more aware of His "ministry of reconciliation."

2. Spend more time on your knees asking God for more opportunities to use this ministry.

3. Ask God to reveal people to whom you can take the ministry of reconciliation, so that old differences can be dealt with and relationships can be restored.

ENGAGE

1. Consider what it means to be an ambassador. Seek opportunities to share the concept with other Christians as an encouragement to them to be involved in the ministry of reconciliation.

2. Spend some time learning the wider truths behind the big words like justification, reconciliation, atonement, appeasement, propitiation, etc. Do word studies using your Bible and Bible helps.

3. Work on being "in the world, but not of the world," so others see that you are different, but not offensive.

Go

1. Take the ministry of reconciliation to a place where it is needed.

2. Think about a wrong you've done that was never made right. Go and pursue reconciliation, even if it means swallowing your pride so you can be a more effective disciple.

Churches

Pray

1. Spend time on your knees as a church, praying that your church will be committed to the ministry of reconciliation.

2. Pray that those holding grudges, or harboring differences and animosity will have the grace and courage to deal with them for Christ's glory, and for the strengthening of the church's testimony.

Engage

1. Does your church have a missions' plan that includes the ministry of reconciliation?

2. Is reconciliation preached from the platform of your church?

3. How could you and other like-minded people in your church encourage the elders and pastoral leaders to focus more on reconciliation?

Go

1. Plan a "Reconciliation Sunday" at your church where the concept is the subject of the whole service, including preaching reconciliation between members who have differences.

2. Focus on helping the whole church to adopt a stronger position on being "in the world but not of the world."

CHAPTER 7

RECTIFY

**How we tend to avoid reality and truth.
Time to clean out the cupboard and rectify myths.**

*"Love is the root of missions;
sacrifice is the fruit of missions."*
— Roderick Davis

*"God is not looking for people of great faith,
but for individuals ready to follow Him."*
— Hudson Taylor

There are some myths around missions and discipling that many are happy to employ and believe. These are stumbling blocks to grasping the need for witnessing locally and disciple-making globally.

Myth: The focus of the Great Commission is only about global missions.
Truth: The Great Commission is about making disciples globally and locally.

For some people missions is a distant, disconnected activity involving brave people who went to some other country. They have their photo posted on a 'Missions Board' in the foyer, and every so often they get welcomed home. For others, it's a case of, 'Why go over there when there is so much need here?'

Missions does not mean we should neglect local outreach. We are commanded to make disciples, and that should most readily play out in the communities in which we live, work and play. In fact, one grows out of the other. The Great Commission is not an 'either/or' option, it is a 'both/and' command, both locally and globally. David Platt explains the difference between unsaved and unreached.[22] Unsaved means people who have heard the good news and refused God's offer. Unreached means "that a group has no access to the gospel - no church, no Christian, no Bible available to them. Practically speaking, if you live among an unreached people group, you will be born, you will live and you will die without ever hearing the gospel that Christians celebrate."[23] Globally in 2016 over two billion people in more than six thousand people groups fell into the unreached category. This is a shocking situation. Our question for you is, "What are you going to do about it?"

Heather Burton's Story

Andrew had finished preaching on missions and the need for global church planting. He had focused on Nepal and a partnership with Niranjan and Sonu Adhikary, an amazing couple who oversee a network of churches and lead a discipleship training program throughout Nepal. Andrew shared with his church that Niranjan and Sonu were going to plant a church which would also be a business center to help fuel the gospel, by providing long-term, sustainable relief to many who suffered through the horrendous earthquakes of 2015. A woman named Heather walked up to Andrew and announced, "I want to be in the two percent." Andrew did a double take. "Excuse me?" Heather said it again: "I want to be among the two percent who go to the unreached parts of the world. Wherever you want to send me, I will go."

Wow. What obedience. What faith. This is the kind of conversation every pastor wishes they could have at the end of a Sunday message. The North American church only sends about two percent of its missionaries to unreached parts of the world.

Only one out of every 1,800 Christians in the "Christian third of the world" decides to serve as a missionary. Out of this number (about 400,000 total), roughly seventy-two percent go to the one-third of the world that is already 'Christian.' The vast majority go to the part of the world with churches. Twenty-five percent of the missionaries go to the one-third of the world that has access to the church, but has chosen not to follow Him yet. That leaves only two or three percent to go the one-third of the world without any chance of hearing about Jesus (Global Frontier Missions).[24] We need more Heather Burtons. We must be willing to give everything away for the gospel.

Myth: The Great Commission is all about evangelism.
Truth: The Great Commission is about evangelism and discipleship.

Jesus gave us the Great Commission, and it was not a command He left open for discussion. Missions = Discipleship. Discipleship is about engaging (the Word), following and obeying (Jesus) and going (making disciples). We believe that missions is as much about discipleship as it is about evangelism. Discipleship is about obedience and intentionally walking with Jesus through the everyday stuff of life.

Matthew's gospel is all about discipleship. He is looking for disciples to live as disciples. So often Christians just claim the title but fail to live the life that Jesus has called them to, or sadly, they have never been taught by the church what it means to truly follow Him. Jesus' call to His disciples isn't to help people just pray some sinner's prayer so they can be saved. We don't find that in the Bible anywhere. His call is for each disciple to die to himself daily. Then Jesus said to His disciples, "Whoever wants to be my disciple must deny themselves and take up their cross and follow me. For whoever wants to save their life will lose it, but whoever loses their life for me will find it" (Matthew 16:24-25).

Discipleship is a process. 1 John 5:3 says, "For this is the love of God, that we keep his commandments. And his commandments are not burdensome." From the very beginning Jesus and His disciples were all about disciple making, pouring their lives into the lives of others. When you read the gospel of Matthew, there is a direct relationship between Matthew 4:19 and Matthew 28:19.

Jesus called out to them, "Come, follow me, and I will show you how to fish for people!" (Matthew 4:19) and "Go make disciples of all nations" (Matthew 28:19). To be a disciple means to make disciples. Making disciples is the overflow of being a disciple. The command that has been given to His disciples is the call for multiplication of disciples: Disciples who make disciples who make disciples. When was the last time you made a disciple?

Myth: The Great Commission is all about going.
Truth: The Great Commission is about making disciples.

The church needs to make the Great Commission part of everyone's personal mission. The mission God has given the church is the same mission He has given every disciple. The 'going' is about the commitment. It is being utterly available to God's direction. For you, 'going' might mean:

- going to your bank account to help fund missions
- going to your email provider to send an encouraging message to someone serving the Lord
- going to your church's mission meeting and offering to help
- going to a place to pray in a detailed and knowing way for someone in missions
- going across the street to mow the neighbor's lawn when they are sick
- going to the supermarket to buy something extra for someone who is housebound
- going to a friend's house party to lend support even when you are tired
- going to visit someone who has lost a loved one
- going to Ecuador to be a full-time missionary

Jesus said, "All authority on heaven and on earth has been given to me" (Matthew 28:18). Here He is declaring that all power, dominion, rule and sovereignty have been given to Him. This authority is given to Jesus by God the Father. Before He gives the mandate He establishes His absolute authority to ensure that the disciples know they can complete the mission under that authority. Then He delivers the mandate: "Therefore GO and make disciples of all nations."

We often get the impression that "go" is the emphasis of the command, but the main verb of the sentence is to "make disciples." This is the imperative verb. This is what our lives must be about. The Greek word for nations, ethne, is where we get the English word 'ethnic' which refers not to modern day geopolitical states, countries or territories but instead to all nations and people groups. Throughout the New Testament we see the spread of the gospel to the ends of the earth. Jesus didn't say, 'Go make disciples only in your city,' though that is important. He didn't say, 'Just stay in your country and go no further.' Jesus has called us and given us the privilege to join Him on mission and to GO into and through the whole world to make disciples who make disciples who make disciples.

How do we make disciples? Jesus tells us by "baptizing them in the name of the Father and of the Son and of the Holy Spirit, and teaching them to obey everything I have commanded you" (Matthew 28:19). We make disciples by baptizing and teaching. Baptism indicates a new identity. We are united into Jesus' death, burial and resurrection. It is a public identification with and surrender to Jesus and the work He has done for salvation. Paul tells us that when we are in Christ, we are made new. "Therefore, if anyone is in Christ, the new creation has come: The old has gone, the new is here!" (2 Corinthians 5:17)

Then we are reminded: "AND SURELY I...." Here Jesus uses the authoritative voice, the Alpha and the Omega, the first and the last, the great I AM, the One who rose from the dead and has commanded you to live on mission with Me, "I am with you always, to the very end of the age" (Matthew 28:20). Who are you with? We like to say we are with our brides - we both married UP! If you meet our wives, you will definitely understand. This is a question often asked in social settings. Who you are with can determine your social status or rank. If people know someone famous they are quick to point out, "I'm with them," or "They're with me." Jesus is with you. Jesus specifically promises to be with us when we are making disciples. It is done in His power and for His glory. How will this get accomplished? Through the power of the Holy Spirit. The disciples had been given the mission, but they must have been concerned as to how on earth they would accomplish it. They had no money, no social network, no power, no support group. There was only one way they were going to do anything - in the power of the Holy Spirit. That's why Jesus told them that He would be with them forever. We will never walk alone. We have the power of the Holy Spirit with us. He is our teacher, comforter, helper and advocate. He will guide us to speak in truth and love.

Myth: The Great Commission is not for me. I am not called to go.
Truth: The Great Commission is a command given to every disciple.

In Acts 1:8, we read "But you will receive power when the Holy Spirit comes on you; and you will be my witnesses in Jerusalem, and in all Judea and Samaria, and to the ends of the earth."

Do you notice a repeating word? Three times we read the word, 'you.' It is personal. God's mission is directed to you. He gives each and every disciple the power of the Holy Spirit. He is personal and active in the life of every disciple, and He gives power to be His witnesses to preach the Word. He gives us the power, ability, strength and words to be witnesses for Jesus.

Witnessing and discipling are not gifts of the Spirit as those mentioned in Romans 12:6, 1 Corinthians 12:4–30, 1 Corinthians 14:1 or 1 Peter 4:10. We all have a gift from God but those gifts differ from Christian to Christian. Alongside

those designated gifts are direct commands like those covered
in the balance of Romans 12 that apply to all Christians.

In the first chapter of Acts Jesus had just resurrected from
the dead. While sitting with His closest friends He told them,
"Do not leave Jerusalem, but wait for the gift my Father
promised, which you have heard me speak about" (Acts 1:4).

Jesus tells them to wait. Waiting is not something that comes
easily. We live in an impatient world, and we are impatient
people. We like to analyze the checkout lines at the supermarket
to see which one will get us through first. We always pick the
path of least resistance, to be in and out as quickly as we can.
Why did the drive-thru get invented? Because walking in and
getting food took too long. A friend of ours hates to wait at
traffic lights, so he will literally go out of his way to get to his
destination before he has to stop at a traffic light. He is never
on time!

Jesus had given His disciples one instruction. Wait. Wait for
help to arrive before you go out and make disciples. By waiting,
they would receive help through the Holy Spirit to be His
witnesses. By waiting, they would receive what they needed to
take the name of Jesus to every nation, tribe, language and
people group. When Jesus was with His disciples He told them
that He must leave so that someone greater could come (John
14). Now what would be better than having Jesus beside you?
Forget your lunch money? No worries! Jesus would produce a
meal for you and you would have enough for the whole week.
Struggling with an injury? Jesus would get you stitched up right
away. Not having any luck catching anything? Jesus would tell
you what side of the boat to throw the line. Your crops are
taking too long to grow? Jesus would put them on the fast path
for growth. Not understanding trigonometry? Jesus would teach
you the real stuff you need to know.

Let Me Tell You a Story (Name changed)

Imagine times are tough and you can only give $5.00 per month. Here's what $5.00 did in the hands of a partner in India who manages sewing classes. Anula was a Hindu, married with three children. She was beaten almost daily by her husband. He was alcoholic, vicious, and abusive in every way. He resorted to sly and unmentionable atrocities against his wife. Anula literally had nothing except two saris and some pots.

She endured the violence for years, but as the children got older, she planned to take her own life, and asked her sister to care for the children. Over several months, Anula saved enough to buy half a gallon of petrol. She planned to burn herself to death on the street in front of her husband's parent's home. She chose a Monday, when her husband would be at his parent's house.

On the Saturday before, a friend who knew about her plight invited her to go to a sewing class run by a Pastor supported by Bright Hope World. She went out of curiosity. For the first time in her life, she was touched, in love by another adult.

The discussion at the class was about a loving Father who sent His Son to die for her. Anula found the story fascinating. Within a couple of weeks, Anula came to Christ, was saved and baptized, led her children to the Lord, and then her husband, who is now fully reformed and remorseful.

I have listened to her testimony as she witnesses to others like an obedient disciple of Jesus. It is powerful and compelling. Others are coming to Christ because of her faithfully told story.

Only $5.00 a month. Never, ever say you cannot afford it.

Jesus was telling His friends that they are to continue on the mission that He gave them, but before they could go and do anything, they needed help. Help was on the way. Jesus was limited to being in one place at one time, but this Helper would be in them everywhere, even to the ends of the earth. A great multiplication would happen only through the power of the Holy Spirit. Jesus had given the commands they were to obey, and through the empowerment of the Spirit these would take place.

Luke uses the same word, "witnesses," to describe us in his version of the Great Commission (Luke 24:44-49). We are the plan for taking the message to those here, near, and all the way over there. We are the ones who are to tell the truth of who God is and what He has done for us. We are to declare the message of a sovereign God who rules, sustains and holds the universe together. We are to share about a loving Father who created each of His children in His image, with meaning and purpose. We are to share about the utter lostness of man due to his sinful ways, who will face an eternal damnation if they don't turn to Christ. We must proclaim the supremacy of Jesus, who can restore, redeem, and recover us from our sinful nature and make us whole again. We are to saturate our neighborhoods, communities and cities with His love until all know.

Common Excuses

We think we've heard almost every excuse there is for not doing missions. Some are novel, some are plain ordinary. Here are a few common ones:

"We don't have any or enough money to give to missions."

There are all sorts of variations around this theme of being too poor to help. Most of us have had times in our lives when money was tight, and giving to the Lord was difficult and a real sacrifice. Invariably though, we can find enough for some of the other things that are not essential - it's usually a matter of priority and whether we value what the Lord has done for us enough to make giving work. We aren't aware of anyone ever going broke or having to sell a business because they gave too much to missions or their church.

What we do want to stress is that a little counts big with God. If we truly are in tight financial circumstances and giving even a small sum is all that is possible, make sure you give that small sum for two reasons. First, you are obeying a biblical command to give something from what you have earned, and God blesses such a sacrifice. Most people know the story of the widow's two mites, and how the Lord was delighted with her small gift because of her sacrifice and attitude.

Secondly, a little goes a long way. We cannot emphasize this enough. A great African proverb says, "Little by little makes a bundle." A dollar goes a long way in most countries. We have seen miracles like the loaves and fishes example achieved with very scant resources. It is not for us to determine what can or can't be done with a small gift. God is not limited. He is more interested in your attitude than your wallet.

"I don't have time."

As with the concern about money, there are still countless things you can do in missions if you are genuinely short of time and finances. You can pray. This costs neither dollars nor days.

There is a huge need for prayer support for discipling. Find a person or the right people in your church or missions organization, and start praying for them by name and by need. Most organizations in missions have a website. Set it as a favorite and click it every morning to find three things you can pray for that day. Pray in the shower, pray driving to school or work, pray while you are at the supermarket. By the way, shutting your eyes to pray is not essential, although it does help with concentration and avoiding distractions.

My daughter-in-law's father was a godly man, who lived to be 93 years old. He actually wore out two spots in the carpet by his bed where he knelt to pray. Almost unbelievable. He had books of names, organizations, and events that he prayed for twice a day. That is diligence and faithfulness. You may not have time to spend by your bed, but you still have time - redeem it.

"I'm not really switched on by missions."

Really? You think God owed you something when He gave His greatest possession - His Son - to die for your sin? You think the overwhelming tide of mercy and grace He has demonstrated to you was what He should have been doing anyway? My friend, go back and spend time reading Ephesians and Philippians and ask God to both forgive you and give you some passion for the lost and those suffering injustice because of the sin in men's hearts. There is a dying and hurting world in your neighborhood and across the globe.

"What can I do when there are so many millions out there needing help?"

We have some sympathy for this reaction, strangely. We sometimes overload people with big statistics that overwhelm us. At times it looks like we are being asked to empty Lake Superior with a bucket. Such a response indicates a possible wrong assumption. God doesn't call us to save the millions - He asks us to make Him known and share what we know with as many as we are able. If you are called to be the next Billy Graham you will be given the tools to achieve such a mission. If your neighbor over the fence needs Christ share your story with him or her. God does the saving. One at a time is good fishing if we all have our lines in the water.

Owen's father taught Sunday School for 44 years in a rather remote corner of New Zealand. He wondered near the end of his days whether he had made a difference. Was it all worthwhile, given there were times when he only had a dozen or so kids to work with? Then one day he received a letter from a woman he had taught many years earlier. She had learned a Bible verse he had given her, but when she moved away from the district, she took no further interest in spiritual things.

One day as she drove past a church, she saw the very same verse on a billboard. She was so arrested by the verse she still remembered, that she turned around and went back to speak to someone in the church, who subsequently led her to faith in Christ. She led her brother to the Lord, and together they went to Africa as missionaries. Her letter to my Dad told stories of leading hundreds of Africans to the Lord, and how God had blessed their work. All my Dad had done was encourage a young girl to learn a Bible verse - God did the rest.

Not a big cost to my Dad, was it? But the Almighty can turn a couple of loaves and some fish into a meal for hundreds - why doubt His ability to take your small contribution and multiply it?

Myth: I have to go to Bible College to be a missionary.
Truth: Anyone can be a missionary.

Anyone can become a full-time or part-time missionary or cross-cultural worker. There are differing means to how it happens, but what will never change is the reason why. We are commanded to make disciples near and far. For some, their global outreach is their home, for some it's their neighborhoods, for others it's their city or state or country and for others it's around the world.

Gone are the days when only those who attended a Bible college or a seminary could become a missionary worker. There are endless opportunities that can open up for people to get involved in serving cross-culturally. Somewhere along your missionary journey, Bible College is an important and useful option. It may not be what you do straight out of high school, but if you are thinking of going into missions you should try to get some training, and a Bible College will set you up well. It will provide you the tools to properly understand, apply and teach the Bible, and give you a deeper understanding of God, Jesus, and the Holy Spirit.

If you are reading this and thinking it's too late to do something missions-minded as a second career, it isn't. There are various ways that you can be effective in reaching the unreached. Despite our resistance, God is patient with us and will use our past experiences to catalyze our futures.

If business is your passion, you may have the opportunity to train business people in a closed country. You might help with microenterprise development in a developing country. If you love medicine, you may be the vessel to provide physical and spiritual healing to unreached people groups. Teachers are able to get into many otherwise closed countries and quietly work for Christ while teaching.

Don't allow the excuses "but" or "when" or "if" to stop you from doing the Lord's work. In Luke 9:57-62, Jesus asks those who want to follow Him to count the cost. It's about being all in, or not at all. Put the world behind us and keep the Word before us. Jesus says that those who follow Him will not live a life of comfort. They may not have a regular street address, let alone a bed. Jesus asks whether His potential

Harry's Priority

It is easy to make time for our so-called priorities. You have an important role to play in God's story. Harry is a plumber in a small New Zealand town. He is not well off but he trusts God and makes missions a priority.

Each year he takes a week off and goes to a third world to help with providing clean water and improved sanitation. Harry isn't well educated but he is obedient to the Lord's command.

He doesn't have a heap of money in the bank but he is building "treasure in heaven".

follower is ready to give up the comforts of home. He then calls for another to follow Him and that man says, "Jesus, just let me wait until things are a little more financially secure." You see, this man's father was still alive. When his father died, he would get his inheritance and be financially secure. Jesus tells him, "Let the dead bury their own dead, but you go and proclaim the Kingdom of God" (Luke 9:60). The next one tells Jesus, "I will follow you, Lord; but first let me go back and say goodbye to my family" (Luke 9:61).

How many times do we say:

"Jesus, I am all about going to church with my family, BUT I can't give up my golf game on Sunday mornings."

"Jesus, I am all about serving You, BUT not during football season."

"Jesus, I want to follow You, BUT I can't give up my current lifestyle."

"Jesus, I know there are orphans in need, BUT I really like watching my cable TV."

It is easy to make time for our so-called priorities. You have an important role to play in God's story. God has made you uniquely you. Fortunately or unfortunately, there is only one of you. God has made you perfectly as He chose. Sadly, we often fail to embrace the way that God has made us. We think we are not good enough or smart enough, then seeds of doubt creep in saying, "I could never be used by God."

May we never underestimate how God can use us for His glory. He will use us for the spreading of His gospel for all to know if we are willing. You are part of God's handiwork. You have a part to play. "For we are God's handiwork, created in Christ Jesus to do good works, which God prepared in advance for us to do" (Ephesians 2:10). It explains we are God's handiwork, His masterpiece. In the Greek, this word is where we get the English word 'poem.' We need to remember that we are fashioned and formed by the Maker of heaven and earth in His own image. We are a masterpiece that is unique, gifted, and commissioned for the sake of His glory to make disciples. He knows you, so trust Him. God is doing a great work in you.

We are all called to full-time ministry, whether we are paid for it or not. Our lives are the gospel. Peter wrote, "Each of you should use whatever gift you have received to serve others, as faithful stewards of God's grace in its various forms" (1 Peter 4:10). We have all been given gifts, not for our own purposes, but for building up the body of Christ.

The Authority of Jesus

One day when Preecha (Andrew's Thai friend) was teaching the Bible, three monks came into the class wearing yellow robes. At first, they sat quietly in the last row of the class. We took a break from my teaching for fifteen minutes. It was a good chance for the monks to ask me many questions about Jesus Christ. They said, "Jesus is just a mere man. He's not God." I showed them the Scriptures stating that Jesus Christ is God.

They showed me a book that spoke against each of the Scriptures of the Bible. Finally, I asked them to show me the Scripture from their holy book that says Buddha is God. They failed to show me. He was just a man who was trying to find the truth, and was a god who was exalted by man. From that day, they put off their yellow robes and came to attend the class. They received baptism in the name of Christ. Now they are effective evangelists among their own people in Thailand.

From the beginning of Scripture, we can clearly see that God created human beings in a special, unique and personal way. On the sixth day of creation, "God said, 'Let us make man in our image, in our likeness...'" (Genesis 1:26). You see, folks, we were created in the image of God, which means we were designed to be vessels of God's greatness. From the moment you were born, actually before you were born, God had a plan for your life. Look at what He says in Jeremiah: "Before I formed you in the womb I knew you, before you were born I set you apart; I appointed you as a prophet to the nations" (Jeremiah 1:5).

It's a deliberate decision to share Jesus as you do life everyday, sitting in the classroom, in the hallway walking to the next business meeting, practicing with your son on the soccer pitch, sitting in a café enjoying a mocha. A disciple will search for the lost and not only agree with the Great Commission, but decide to live in it and through it daily.

You have something to offer. Don't listen to the world - it will tell you otherwise. Instead, tap into the Word. The Apostle Paul wrote to the church in Corinth, sharing how everyone has a part to play in God's Kingdom:

"But God chose the foolish things of the world to shame the wise; God chose the weak things of the world to shame the strong...... so that no one may boast before him. It is because of him that you are in Christ Jesus, who has become for us wisdom from God - that is, our righteousness, holiness and redemption" (1 Corinthians 1:27-30).

In Defense of Your Faith

Peter put it this way: "But in your hearts, set apart Christ as Lord. Always be prepared to give an answer to everyone who asks you to give the reason for the hope that you have. But do this with gentleness and respect" (1 Peter 3:15).

If you are going to defend your faith or give a useful answer, you need a method. If you strike interest with your own story, you can take a person along the "Romans Road":

1. Romans 3:23 shows them their need to realize they are sinners, and that their sin separates them from God.
2. Romans 6:23 tells them the consequences of sin.
3. The same verse opens the door for hope.
4. Romans 5:8 tells us what God has done to fix our problem.
5. Romans 10:9 explains what we must do.
6. Romans 10:13 confirms the transaction.

God can use you. What is your excuse for why God can't use you? We all come up with them, either to get out of things we don't like or things we think we can't do. It is important to note that when Jesus called the disciples to follow Him (Matthew 4:19), the disciples were not at that time what Jesus wanted them to be. The Gospels reveal that these men were:

- blue collar workers like fishermen
- poor
- uneducated

- selfish
- self-centered
- often quick-tempered
- proud
- weak
- cowardly
- frail

They were not perfect, but Jesus promised to "make" them to "become" fishers of men. He will do the same in you, if you let Him shape and mold you for His glory.

The "go" in this instance is going to set up such projects, monitoring them and ensuring prayer support. It can be done by part-timers who are plumbers or accountants for eleven months of the year in Dallas or Detroit, Wellington or Washington.

Myth: I don't need to share the gospel with words. Actions speak louder.
Truth: We need to use words when sharing the gospel.

An earnest disciple will naturally develop a hunger and passion to share God's love and grace to a hurting and lost world. We are called to evangelize, and the most effective method of evangelism is through sharing the gospel verbally. We must never downplay the importance of communicating the truth of the Scriptures. Many say, "I just live a good life and others will come to Christ that way." They use the example of what St. Francis of Assisi said: "Preach the gospel; when necessary, use words." This makes the message incomplete. Words are vital to give a true gospel presentation.

Be prepared

If you were asked to give a speech at school, you may wing it just to get through the class. Been there, done that! If you were asked to give a presentation to your boss at work, you'd at least put some effort into learning the information for the presentation. If you were asked to present in front of a large crowd or at a convention, you would ensure you knew the subject very well. We need to be in the Word to be able to share it effectively "For the mouth speaks out of that which fills the heart" (Matthew 12:34).

Have confidence

Often we think we don't have anything worth sharing. If our salvation is only a ticket to heaven and our Christian life is barren and unexciting, witnessing could do more damage than good. Be yourself. Tell your story, warts and all. Don't try to share something you haven't experienced. Remember, you are a "witness." It's about what you have felt, known and learned. Keep it simple, real and unforced. Practice makes perfect, so use a role model. Try witnessing in front of your Christian support group. Create lots of potential situations and keep practicing until you feel comfortable with your own voice and your subject. Jesus had His disciples practice (Matthew 10). Practice as though lives depend on you - because they do.

Keep growing

Most importantly, keep praying and learning. Pray for opportunities, pray for wisdom and strength to be effective and God-honoring, pray for the right words and sensitivity, pray that the Holy Spirit will use your efforts and pray for the person to be followed up as they come to Christ.

Some think they need to get their own life in order before they start witnessing. They think that someday they will reach a level of maturity where they will be effective. Sorry, but that is not going to happen, ever. Jesus doesn't need perfect witnesses. If He did, we would never get to do it. Some of the most powerful witnessing is done by new Christians overflowing with excitement and newfound contentment in Christ.

Witnessing at a personal level can be challenging and sometimes traumatic. I (Owen) remember being sent as a teenager by an overzealous pastor who was keen for us to do cold calling and witnessing. He sent us into a small mining town dominated by tough miners. On two doorsteps I got told in very colorful, vigorous language to "get back out the gate and put your @#&!!* religion ...!" I was petrified. Nothing was gained. It was not very smart thinking on the part of the pastor.

Although cold encounters can be fruitful and never lost, the more strategic and biblical way to witness is through existing relationships. I have experienced great one-off opportunities on aircraft, for example, where jammed into a seat with a stranger for hours on end sharing something of Jesus' love in my life was a very special thing. At least a couple of these encounters have led to ongoing relationships, where more fruitful discussions have ensued. Never miss an opportunity, remembering that it is the Holy Spirit that does the saving - all we have to do is witness to the saving mercy of the Lord.

It is important to note that an essential but often overlooked ingredient in becoming a Christian is repentance. Saying sorry is so hard. However, it is critical to becoming a Christian (Acts 20:21, Matthew 4:17, Luke 5:32). Too often, we try to help sinners come to Christ by trying to make it as easy as possible.

Repentance seems like a big obstacle they might not want to get over, but there is great danger in 'easy believism.' Repentance is "granted by God" (2 Timothy 2:25), and no one comes to the knowledge of salvation unless the Father draws them (John 6:44).

Some well-meaning pastors have led Christians to believe that you must develop a relationship with people in order to earn the 'right' to share the good news with them. They say, "People will not care about what you have to say until they know you care." Or, "You shouldn't shove the gospel down people's throats." First of all, there is no "right" to preach the gospel of Christ. It is a simple command and we use whatever situation and tools we have, lacing our words with grace and sensitivity. There is no right way or preconditions needed, although building friendships clearly helps.

We must remember that evangelism is a process. It takes time to bring people to the point in which they accept Jesus as Savior and Lord. Evangelism is not a program of the church - it is the role of every disciple. "As for you, always be sober-minded, endure suffering, do the work of an evangelist, fulfill your ministry" (2 Timothy 4:5, ESV). The call from Paul to Timothy is to "do the work of an evangelist." Timothy was not called to be an evangelist: rather, he was told to do the work of an evangelist. This means not only should he minster to those in the church, but he should also have concern for the lost.

Friends, evangelism is the responsibility of each of us. We speak for Christ when we plead, "Come back to God!" In His Sermon on the Mount, Jesus told His disciples how they are to live: "You are the salt of the earth" (Matthew 5:13), "You are the light of the world" (Matthew 5:14). Notice what Jesus says right off the bat. He told His disciples, "You are salt and light." He doesn't say:

- If you want to
- If it suits you
- If you have time to decide
- If you could

No, He tells us, "You are salt and you are light."

To the average person, salt and light may not sound very significant, but these elements possess great power and have a radical influence on whatever they come into contact with. Salt was a very common substance in the ancient world. Roman soldiers were paid in it, and it carried a high level of value. Salt is seen as a powerful tool, and it served many purposes. It was used as a preservative, healer and as an agent to enhance the flavor in cooking. Salt means a preserving influence of all that is right, good, honorable and from above. Salt also makes people thirsty. Jesus is saying to use what we are to show people a different way to live. He wants us to make people thirst for the truth, and thirst for God and His love. We are able to heal those who are in need of a Savior. Jesus said we are to be Salt and Light.

A light is to shine bright. To be an irresistible force that shines through the nothingness of darkness every time. Light has the power to illuminate and expose. Jesus is saying that we are to live a life that illuminates the truth of who He is, through the everyday stuff of life. We are to draw people to Him, the source of all truth, and love and help people come into the light. Jesus declared, "I am the light of the world. If you follow me, you won't have to walk in darkness, because you will have the light that leads to life" (John 8:12, NLT). Salt and light understand what the real issues are from an eternal perspective. They want their lives to be used for the Kingdom and for God's glory.

Jesus was saying to those folks and to us who are Kingdom citizens: "You are My marketing plan. I'm not going to develop an iPhone app, create some Facebook group, or join Twitter and provide the hashtag #gobesaltandlight. No, you are it." Friends, we have the privilege of taking the name of Jesus to the lost in our neighborhoods, workplaces, schools, and never forget the most important place of all - the hallways of your homes.

One Message Multiplied – One Soul Saved Becomes Thousands

India is an amazing country full of contrasts. It is one of the most spiritually dark and desolate countries, with a maze of Eastern religions. Yet there are incredible stories of Christian victories, souls saved, and ministries established.

The population of India is over 1.2 billion. Of the 2,142 people groups, 1,929 are unreached.[iii] Over 80% of the people of India claim Hinduism as their religion. In the Hindu religion, there are over 330 million deities of gods and goddesses. That is more than the population of America. Evangelical Christianity makes up less than 1% of the country's population. Many say it is unknown, due to it being so small in number. Think about that for a moment. The country that will soon be the most populous nation has so few who know the truth of Jesus.

Jay Henry grew up with a Christian father and mother. At one point in time, his grandfather was a Hindu. A faithful missionary who came to India introduced Jay's granddad to Jesus. The granddad then taught his son who then taught his son and sent him to Sunday school. It was Jay's grandmother and Sunday school teacher who shared the gospel with him, leading him to accepting Christ and committing his life to the call of the gospel. His Sunday School teacher then baptized him.

In one of the darkest countries in the world Jay and his wife Romola are bringing light through their mission Mid India Christian Mission. In 1969, Dr. Vijai Lall, Romola's brother, along with other members of his family, founded Mid-India Christian Mission with the start of the Nav-Jagriti Christian Day School. Over time, the work grew to include other support for India's Christians. In 1969, Dr. Jay Henry joined Dr. Vijai Lall at the inception of Mid-India Christian Missions and has been involved with the work ever since. Jay helped to establish the mission and is one of the founding members.

Jay was instrumental in many of the mission's projects, including the eye hospital and the day school. He is currently the director of the board, and teaches full-time at the Bethlehem Bible College. Through this Bible College they have graduated over 500 preachers. Every single one of these preachers is still in ministry today, despite many having been kicked out of their families for claiming Jesus as their Lord and Savior. Several of the preachers are not able to return home because they follow Christ. If Jay and Romola can do this in a country where they are constantly in danger, facing persecution and hardship, what is our excuse?

Rectify
Chapter Reflections

Individuals

Pray

1. Spend time on your knees asking God to help you live radically, passionately and sacrificially for His gospel to go to the ends of the earth.

2. Ask God what gifts He has given you and how you can advance the gospel by using these gifts.

3. Pray for God to give you an awareness of needs, both locally and globally. Pray about what part you might play in reaching people with God's gospel.

Engage

1. What myths have you believed about the Great Commission? What perceptions or understanding of theology need to change?

2. When have you underestimated how God can use you for His glory?

3. How can you and your family give generously toward unreached people groups and change the 1% of missions funds being sent to the unreached?

Go

1. How are you being utterly available to God's direction? Where is He calling you to go and be His messenger?

2. What excuse or excuses have you been giving God regarding why you can't be involved in seeing His gospel spread globally?

Churches

Pray

1. Spend time on your knees for people in your church and for the leaders of your church to overcome excuses like "but" or "when" or "if" that can stop them from engaging in missions.

2. Pray for your church to obey and accept the fact that God has commanded us to be part of reaching people for Christ, and that this is the purpose of the church.

3. Spend time on your knees asking for your church to be intentional about listening to the Holy Spirit, to be led by the Holy Spirit, and empowered though the Holy Spirit.

Engage

1. How is your church helping your people not just "try" to be good witnesses, but to be trained, equipped, and deployed for sharing their faith?

2. Evangelism is not a program of the church - it is the role of every disciple. The mission of the church is to win lost souls for Jesus. How is this embedded into the culture of your church?

3. How is your church helping people grow in their understanding of the gospel that forms and fuels disciples to be sent into the world?

Go

1. Help your church to see how they can use their gifts to serve others. We have all been given gifts, not for our own purposes, but for building God's Kingdom locally and globally.

2. Are there areas of your city, maybe communities that are unreached or are populated by differing ethnic groups where you could send your church to engage in being witnesses for Jesus? Is your church active in universities in your city where you can engage with others by being witnesses for Jesus? If not, what are the obstacles that would prevent this, and how can you overcome them?

Chapter 8

Represent

**A real world example representing
effective, Bible-based, global missions.**

*"Do not go where the path may lead,
go instead where there is no path and leave a trail."*
– Ralph Waldo Emerson

"Every successful enterprise has a very clear strategic purpose."
– Mitch Daniels, President of Purdue University

Bright Hope World (BHW)

Bright Hope World (BHW) is based in New Zealand. It is small by world standards. Their annual budget would be less than what some international ministries spend in a month. We contend that size does not matter. Nor does the number of missionaries in the field matter, nor the number of "souls saved and recorded in the KPI's or the annual report," nor the names of the heavyweights on the advisory board, nor the number of sponsored children hiding under fridge magnets - although they all may be helpful at times. What does matter is the obedience, motivation, passion, focus and Christ-inspired, biblical technique.

The BHW story is not unique, entirely. Thankfully, there are dozens of missions organizations out there working hard, taking risks, trusting the Lord, and seeing discipling happen every day. However, BHW serves our purpose for proposing a different way of doing missions. There are techniques and ideas you can and should copy. You can learn more about them on their website at www.brighthopeworld.com. Rob Purdue, who started BHW with his wife Heather, wants any mention of Bright Hope World to be about God, His Spirit's work, the command of Christ, and how amazing Bright Hope partners are changing their world. "Focus on the partners", he demanded. "They are the giants of faith and commitment. Focus on the team that God graciously gave me." So we will.

Partner Example 1: Subong

Subong has a rustic little sign at his gate. It reads, "Bright Hope Nagaland." Behind the sign is his small two-acre farm, perched on the hillside. Nagaland has very little flat land.

You may be wondering where Nagaland is. Rob certainly did when he first met Subong in Bangalore on a visit to India. Nagaland is a state in northeast India, tucked around past Bangladesh, next to Myanmar - a very beautiful mountainous area that was evangelized in the 1870's by American Baptists. There are many Christians in Nagaland as a result of the diligence and sacrifice of the early missionaries. However, there has also been a disturbing falling away and loss of effectiveness in the church. Young people were no longer interested in the Christianity of their grandparents. This concerned Subong, himself a Naga. It is also a poor area, especially outside of the towns.

BHW was impressed by Subong's passion. He quickly laid out his plans. He had a little piece of land just outside Dimapur, the second largest town in Nagaland. Could Bright Hope World help him turn it into a viable demonstration farm?

Rob wondered about the merit of the idea. Some background checks on Subong revealed his sincerity, commitment and ability. The BHW team sought guidance from the Lord - but Rob wanted to be sure. He took his time, watching and learning. Rob concluded that Subong was a man of integrity and would know what would work best in his home patch. He was investing God-given resources in a person, not a project.

He listened carefully as Subong laid out his ideas for his small piece of land. It was time to create a partnership that treated Subong as a genuine, equal partner.

The whole story deserves another chapter in another book, but for now we'll tell you that Subong converted his little farm into an ideal demonstration unit. He used his space to show others what must be done to prevent erosion from the all-too-popular subsistence farming in Nagaland, which filled the local rivers with silt and destroyed the land. Subong now has vegetables and nut trees at the higher end of his little farm, cows, pigs, ducks and chickens along the side of the hill and a fish pond at the bottom of the slope.

All the animal and vegetable waste is pushed down the hill to the fish, a type of carp that eat everything except plastic bags. The carp grow to edible size within six months. The fish are harvested, the pond is drained, and the rich nutrients dug from the bottom of the pond go up to the vegetable plot and grassland for the cows. Subong has created an enclosed sustainable operation focused on producing protein, which is sorely needed for a balanced diet to complement the ever-present rice.

What did Bright Hope World Like about Subong?

1. He was genuine and sincere.
2. He had researched the issues and was capable and knowledgeable.
3. He had a passion and long-term vision for his people.
4. He knew how to make a combined commercial and evangelical project work.
5. He had formed an advisory group of trained specialists to help and provide accountability.
6. The project had the ability to be independent of BHW's support in a short time.

The farm is now a permanent, erosion-proof, viable unit. Trees are encouraged, not cut down, and the land is stabilized. Other farmers who move from plot to plot and have watched the soil slide into the river below no longer have to follow a dangerous subsistence farming method. These are the rivers that carry tons of silt down to Bangladesh, causing widespread flooding and loss of life.

More importantly, every Friday, Subong holds a demonstration day and invites very poor farmers from all over Nagaland to see his farm operation, learn improved, more profitable, safer farming methods, then hear a clear gospel message - practical and effective ministry. Subong loves sharing the message of Jesus' love, and he has the respect of his listeners. Farm profits help support a local Bible school instructing young converts.

New Techniques

Bright Hope World has adopted some highly effective but simple farming systems that are transforming agriculture in places like Africa and Southeast Asia.

The techniques were initially developed by Foundations for Farming in an attempt to revolutionize agriculture in Africa. Past efforts have not worked well. Despite over $2 billion U.S. dollars spent on aid in Africa in the last 10 years, poverty numbers and average crop yields have deteriorated.

Foundations for Farming and BHW are using zero tillage, no burning, composting, and other low cost, easy-to-adopt and teach methods that are radically increasing yields, improving water retention, and enhancing soil fertility while creating jobs and well-being.

This is discipling at a practical level.

Key Elements in the Nagaland Missions Program

Relationships

BHW started by building relationships. The investment is in people, not projects. It took time to build the relationships, carefully checking the partners-to-be, making sure they were of good character, that they had leadership skills, and that they were held in esteem locally so their influence could be effective. God's money needs accountability and transparency. Relationships are the essence of evangelism at home and in the mission field. Jesus did not set up a large church. He invested in a few leaders by building a productive and mutually respectful relationship. Christ looked for passion, not performance, nurturers, not numbers, sincerity, not scholarship.

Western Solutions

I (Owen) was watching a group of Indian farmers plough their rice field using one buffalo and a single furrow plough with a shallow ploughshare. I dug around and quickly realized they had a major problem with a hard pan just below the furrow depth. Break that pan, and yields would increase dramatically. I showed them how to change the angle of the share so it ripped the pan open and allowed rice roots to go deeper.

They reluctantly nodded agreement. However, the buffalo did not have the strength to pull the newly changed plough. I had an answer for that, too. After all, I was a successful Western farmer! Simply pull the plough with two buffalo. Sullenly, they set up a tandem team and sure enough, the new idea worked. I went off feeling very satisfied. That's how you do missions successfully!

The next day, we went past the field and to my surprise and hurt pride, the farmer was back to one buffalo. I asked my partner, "Why?" "Simple," he replied, "they can only afford one buffalo."

Respect

There was respect for Subong as a local leader. He was a person of influence who knew what he wanted to do but lacked the resources. When Bright Hope showed Subong respect by treating him as an equal, so did the locals. He was listened to with a new aura around him. Rob believes that God called him to be a servant, not a specialist adviser. Too often, missions is based on a "we know best" approach, indicating a paternalistic or even a colonialist attitude that yields little fruit. It estranges the very people who need to know the life-changing effect of the gospel message.

Rewarding Partnerships

A partnership of mutual respect and equality was formed with Subong. The best person to reach the local people is a respected local person. They know the language, the customs and traditions. They know the opportunities and the threats. Mostly all they need is tools. BHW does not tell people what to do. It does not have a big staff of experts and advisers. The knowledge is already held and only requires stimulation and some technology transferred where new methods are available.

It is sad to see some missions dictating what should happen. They take their knowledge and techniques from home and force feed the locals. They do not take the time to listen, build relationships, identify the genuine leaders, understand the needs, or learn the customs and traditions. The local people are so grateful for attention and that "something" is happening, so they do not raise any objections. They say the right things and smile so the missionary or the missions team feel they are doing the right thing. Programs can run for years with little benefit and few lives changed before it dawns on the mission that they are on the wrong track.

Responsibility

Subong, as the local leader, took responsibility for spreading Christ's message and supporting a discipling project. He was also committed to working with the poorest of the poor. BHW had taken the time to make sure he was the ideal person for the task. Careful accounting and reporting to BHW is done by email and devices like dated photographs, with occasional visits.

Robust Results

The outcomes withstand close scrutiny. They are holistic in nature, seeking to improve the environment while increasing yields, enhancing employment opportunities, making diets better and more wholesome, utilizing resources wisely and strengthening communities. This creates a stable, lasting and effective platform for sharing Christ's love and saving grace.

This project is now complete. No further inputs or resources are needed. BHW seeks such projects where it can trigger a change led by the locals, but soon hand it over to the competent leaders to manage going forward. Too many missions get locked into projects and cannot find a way out. That makes no sense in practical, financial or sustainable terms.

Bright Hope World Distinctives

1. Genuine Partnership: The Cornerstone of Bright Hope World

The essence of BHW is partnership. A carefully managed, prayerfully checked relationship. The modus operandi is to identify local leaders who have integrity, a record of achievement, and a passionate vision for their people, then equip them to achieve their vision. There is rarely, if ever, a community in a developing country that does not have a leader, a person whose character and demeanour is such that they have influence and recognition. BHW has many methods for identifying these strong personalities, then begins a period of checking their suitability. One source of leaders is the South Asia Institute of Advanced Christian Studies (SAIACS) in Bangalore, India.

SAIACS was founded by a New Zealander, Dr. Graham Houghton, a man of vision, strength, and the highest standards in all aspects of his life. The people who study at SAIACS are usually leadership material. BHW calls there every couple of years and meets those who have an interest.

Many new partners have come through existing partners and their contacts. Some have heard of the work and make contact themselves. Some contacts come through Kevin and Helen Honore, who were missionaries in Africa for several years and who have a network among local Christian leaders in central Africa. Kevin is the Field Director of BHW and is responsible in many ways for the success of BHW's partnerships. He is very practical, having owned and managed businesses earlier in his life. Kevin has an amazingly calm and capable manner for talking to partners where he is highly respected. They respect him because he respects them, and treats them as equals in every way. There is not a trace of paternalism or undervaluing - common occurrences which stifle so much global mission activity. Kevin quietly fits into any situation with grace, but with a loving firmness if required. His life is an object lesson on how to work in the field and obtain God-honoring progress.

The process of checking candidates may take up to three years, to ensure BHW has the right person. The checking is obviously about their honesty, their integrity, and their acceptance in the local community, but also focuses heavily on their passion for making changes, their willingness to sacrifice everything to make their plans work, their perseverance to see it through and their love for their people. BHW is looking for people with a track record of serving their community even in small ways. That is vital - if a partner has not performed in the past, there is reason to question whether they will in the future. Humility is not a typical characteristic in India because of the pernicious caste system, but when it is discovered, it is powerful and effective. The amazing thing is that these leaders are not that hard to find. Given the right help, they can achieve great things - far greater than any Westerner could achieve. They rarely under-perform.

Effective Partnerships

Genuine, effective partnerships are based on the belief that the parties have equal value - before God and in terms of capability. Effective partnerships recognize that a local person with a vision for, and commitment to, serving those around them will be far more effective than someone coming in from a foreign culture. Effective partnerships believe that local solutions to local problems will tend to be more successful and sustainable than imported concepts that fail to understand the nuances of local conditions, culture and traditions.

The agency's role is to provide accountability, oversight, and resources, not to be the source of the "bright ideas." Sometimes outside ideas can seem to be accepted because the local people are too well-mannered to say "no" or point out their weaknesses - but invariably they fail. While this concept is relatively easy to accept at face value, it can easily be eroded in practice. In the absence of genuine humility and appreciation for the vision and giftings that God provides to people around the world, partnership fails.

BHW jealously guards its partners because they are the most essential element of the ministry. Too often, well meaning visitors from the developed world arrive and want to impose what they think are obvious solutions and quick fix ideas. It can take months to repair damage done by such ill-conceived initiatives. Consider this small example: A group visiting India decided to take used soft toys to an Indian BHW project. They had hundreds of secondhand toys donated, found an airline that didn't charge overweight fees, and arrived in town with bags of goodies. A quick count showed they had more than enough. Distribution started. The look of sheer delight and awe on the kids' faces was worth the effort. Suddenly, what began as a group of 150 kids become 250, then 350. Word got around quickly. The supply ran out. Kids started climbing over one another to get a toy. Fights broke out. There were tears and yelling. Parents joined in. Disaster. It took months for the local partner to sort out the mess. The kids and parents were not to blame - it was an inappropriate gesture, well meaning but ill-considered.

Once a partnership is initiated, the commitment is long-term. Fast results and returns are not the focus, but rather the ability of the partner to deliver holistic transformation of their local community over a long period of time. BHW will stay involved with the partner until impact is seen and support is no longer required, ideally because the project is completely self-sustaining.

The value of establishing and maintaining these genuine partnerships is impossible to overstate. Unfortunately, too many individuals and agencies treat needy people in developing countries with a degree of arrogance. They may not mean to do so but it happens too often.

What Do Bright Hope World Partners Look Like?

BHW seeks partners who exhibit a number of vital characteristics. These traits are applauded and fostered carefully. The essence of good discipling is to nurture, encourage, and grow Christlikeness so those elements can be handed on to the next generation of disciples.

1. BHW seeks partners who serve out of deep conviction, love, compassion, and an empathy with their village people and their needs. They identify underlying and long-term needs as opposed to immediate needs.. BHW and their partners seek to

identify long-term, underlying problems, and find partners who will commit to a long-term solution and stay in their community for a long period to achieve a sustainable result.

Bright Hope World's relationship with George and Jacqueline Atido in the Congo demonstrates this type of partnership. Both George and Jacqueline are well-trained and educated, and they have decided that the best way of dealing with the deep-seated problems in their area is to work with the next generation. The AIDS epidemic, which is still rife in Africa and leaving numerous orphans, has created an opportunity for George and Jacqueline to focus on providing them food and shelter, but more particularly with a sound general education and Christian training. Most of these children would never get to school otherwise. George and Jacqueline have a long-term plan and are happy looking ahead 20 or 30 years, when better educated, young Christians can step up and take leadership roles.

It costs $155 per child per year to give each one a new start in life and expose them to the gospel message.

2. BHW seeks partners who are multi-dimensional. They are people who have studied the needs of their people and can see what projects are going to do the most for their community over the longer term. It is important to avoid having all the eggs in one basket as disease, war or crop failure may take out one form of income in any given year. The locals know this and seek a range of solutions that they can effectively manage. They identify opportunities that are sustainable and cost-effective, and that if required can be carried on without BHW input. They operate holistically and sustainably.

A good example is Niranjan and Sonu Adhikary in Nepal. Niranjan grabbed the attention of BHW when he was studying at SIAICS in Bangalore. He had the gleam in his eye and the intense focus that cannot be missed. He had plans for his people. He knew exactly what he wanted to do, and why - and the why is vital. The Adhikarys have established a medical clinic in an area with huge problems that had no health facilities, clean water or sanitation for villages. They planted over hundred churches that are flourishing and are well established doctrinally, after starting with just six people in one church. They have set up training programs for a wide range of activities for men, women and young people. They set up a farmers' co-op to help get better returns. Niranjan manages his own revolving microfinance fund for the poorest of the poor, and runs chicken farms to produce revenue for his staff and other Christian workers. If BHW disappeared tomorrow nothing would change, as Niranjan and Sonu have the start they need, are operating on a self-sustaining basis, and are expanding the Kingdom in amazing ways.

3. BHW seeks partners who are people-focused, not project-focused. Many fine sounding projects are placed before the BHW staff each year, but they can be weak on their people impact. Conversely, those opportunities that are likely to impact a large number of people are likely to gain support.

A good example of a funded program that fits this criterion is the work of James and Gorret Bwire in Uganda. James is the headmaster of a school, CEO of a large and successful microloans program that helps families across a range of activities, pastor of a church of over 200 people, and a church planter in surrounding districts. He works closely with the leadership of these churches to ensure they stay focused on the Word of God. Gorret looks after their own family, cares for other children orphaned by AIDS, works in the microloan program, teaches loan recipients how to manage the money and get the best from their loan and is in charge of accountability. Their impact on the poor is significant.

4. Authenticity is paramount in the choice of partners. BHW does not send missionaries, although it does not necessarily oppose the concept of Westerners going to developing countries when they know God is calling them to do so.

A very general comparison, not always true of every situation:

Local Full- or Part-Time Worker	Foreign Missionary
Costs about $1,500 to $2,000 per year	Costs $30,000 to $120,000 a year
No major overheads	Many hidden costs for supporting church
Already knows the language	Has to learn the language
Already knows the culture	Has to learn and adapt to the culture
Has an understanding of what is needed and will work	Has to discern what is needed and will work
No acceptance issues	Often faces acceptance problems
Is on the job all the time	Needs furlough or a substitute

However, there is an important role for both. What we need is better evaluation before resources are committed to either.

2. Field-driven: How That Really Works

Coupled closely with genuine partnerships is the concept of being field-driven. Again, it seems a simple straightforward notion, but it is significantly more complex and vital than it appears. The opposite of field-driven is donor-driven, a trap that can cause endless problems. While donors are critically important and should be respected for their sacrifice and interest in missions, the focus must be heavily on the donee.

It is not unusual for donors to want to control what happens to their money, despite their also claiming they are giving the money to the Lord. This can bring difficulties of confusion and embarrassment leading to all parties losing respect. BHW believes its role is one of an enabler and a point of accountability. It is almost a defining principle of Western society that whoever has the money has the influence. BHW seeks to protect partners in the field from this notion. While large donors are certainly welcome, and BHW seeks to accommodate the needs and requests of these donors, this is never done at the expense of the needs of the partners in the field.

As a general rule, BHW will only take key leaders and potential leaders on visits to the field with a BHW team member present at all times. This is not an issue of trust, but of experience. The potential and history of problems arising in the field during field visits is high, as people operating out of their comfort zones and experiencing strong emotions can easily say or do something which can threaten the partnership or damage the credibility of BHW or the partner in the field. BHW also believes that excessive field visits can lead partners to develop a growing dependency on external input.

Every issue is tested against "how does it affect the partner?" The primary loyalty and focus must remain on the field, and every decision must be considered in the light of its potential impact on our partners in the field. Partners take precedence over everything else.

The nature of missions can easily lead to a well meaning attitude that those doing Christian mission are there to "sort things out", "get these people up to speed", "show them how to do stuff" or "drag them into the real world." It may appear to work, but inevitably it leads to problems. Respect for partners and humility are vital.

3. Accountability

Accountability runs in several directions. In the first instance, in missions and discipling, we are all accountable to God for what He has blessed us with (Romans 14:12). More talents and more responsibility means greater accountability. Then BHW suggests we are accountable to the partner. The BHW team pour their very life into making sure the partner is protected, helped, and served to the best of their ability. Finally, there is accountability to donors and prayer supporters.

Accountability is about openness, transparency, and truthfulness. It's about knowing where your responsibilities lie. Paul said to the Colossians he was a servant or steward of the gospel (Colossians 1:25). The Greek word for steward would have been well known to the Colossians. Often stewards had very great duties, caring for an owner's entire business for long periods of time. Much was expected of them. When the master returned, they endured a rigorous accounting for their responsibilities. In 2 Corinthians 8:20-21 Paul wrote, "taking precaution that no one should discredit us in our administration of this generous gift, for we have regard for what is honorable, not only in the sight of the Lord, but also in the sight of men" (NASB). Accountability to God and men. BHW has strong processes in place at all levels to ensure accountability.

4. Low Overheads

It can be very frustrating to give money to what seems a good cause, only to find that the overheads are taking a very large percentage of what you have given. Some Christian groups appear to have little conscience about taking very high percentages, based on high wages, extensive travel, high class hotels and the like. Overheads of forty percent or more are sadly not uncommon.

When Rob set up BHW, he was adamant that overheads would not exceed ten percent. Through careful planning and a number of initiatives, BHW has been able to ensure that many gifts received have been spent 100% in the field. This has helped to strengthen the donor base over the years. Rob Purdue has used his commercial abilities to invest wisely in property and related opportunities using his own resources, so that the returns could cover the cost of administration.

5. Outcome Focused

A common failing in commercial ventures as well as Christian missions is to become bogged down in process at the expense of achieving the desired outcomes. Over many years business has refined management techniques, commercial operations and quality processes. As this refinement grew, business leaders, CEO's, foremen, and boards of directors became more and more enamored with the process, as opposed to an outcome. They lost sight of achieving the goal as cost effectively and practically as possible. 'Process' has become embedded in many Christian ministries, causing a lack of focus and accomplishment. Partners in developing countries become disillusioned and lose respect and appreciation for the funding partner. BHW operates a very disciplined approach to ensure that projects are set up with strategic objectives, and processes are in place to maintain a close eye on their delivery.

6. Sustainability and Independence

One of the key principles adopted at BHW is to achieve sustainability in its projects. Each project is considered on the basis of how it contributes to improving environmental outcomes, enhancing the social and economic environment, and whether the outcomes will produce a more independent community freed from the shackles of handouts. The developing world is awash with examples of how "aid" has wrecked local economies and made whole communities and regions dependent on the next handout. Christians, as stewards of God's creation, need to take care that what we promote is consistent with His glory being seen in all He has made. That doesn't mean being pantheistic or extreme - it simply means following basic principles of good management of natural resources. Projects that involve microloans and microenterprise and create opportunities to enhance the dignity of the partners are favored over those that require ongoing contributions.

7. Training Essential

A major thrust of BHW's work is to train partners in new techniques, and in turn, to equip those trained to pass on the training in their own communities. A significant number of BHW projects fund suitable trainers because of the obvious benefits to a new generation, that include the ability to share the gospel, discipling as Jesus required and passing on the baton of practical knowledge. This is disciples producing disciples, who produce disciples. There is a deliberate strategy to work their way out of a job, letting the locals take responsibility for their future.

8. Commercial Focus

One of the unusual success features of BHW has been the continuing use of strong commercial imperatives. Not only is BHW supported by a number of commercial businesses that have produced good returns over the years, but partners are encouraged to look for commercial opportunities that can help make their ministry independent and no longer requiring developing world input.

A clever example is Vidya Sagar in Bangalore. He had a recipe for a balm that he claimed was an excellent medicinal product capable of curing a wide range of local problems. He had been given the recipe by his aged uncle. It was certainly a very powerful ointment with several BHW leaders trying it out and quickly wiping it off as it felt too hot on their lighter skin.

Vidya Sagar had a plan. He wanted to build a small factory to manufacture the balm. His idea was to sell it to Indian Christian workers, of which there are many thousands. He would make a small profit from the sales to support his family and a Christian school he was building. The Christian workers were then encouraged to sell the balm to the public using the balm as a way to introduce the gospel - the 'balm for the soul'. That way the workers could support themselves and their families, multiplying the value of the initial investment in the ointment factory.

Vidya Sagar produced the balm for three rupees and sold it for six rupees, while the workers could get nine or ten rupees from the public. There are over 60 rupees in a dollar so it does not sound like a very profitable operation, but in India, a couple of rupees go a long way. This little factory is the means of many Indian people coming to Christ and being discipled. Vidya Sagar and his wife Ruth now have a large Christian school in Bangalore, where children are taught to a high standard and learn about a loving God who offers them eternal life. They know the value of having been discipled and are doing the same to a new generation.

9. Self-Funded Element

Over the years, BHW has raised a significant amount of money from its own investments and operations. Because farming is a profitable venture in New Zealand, some $180,000 was invested in a rundown sheep farm. It was converted into three dairy farms and later sold for over $5 million. There are a number of other investments yielding a return that BHW is able to use to cover its administration costs and contribute to various projects. While the model is not suitable in many situations, it does show the value in having independent funding that smooths out the humps and hollows of "outside" giving that is subject to a number of influences.

10. Promoting a Bi-Vocational Approach

It may take a lot of swallowing, but BHW has no paid staff. Many of the field staff have full-time jobs and operate in the evenings and in their own vacations. Some are self-employed or have work that allows them to be away a little more often. The operating style of careful selection of partners, having clear goals and modern communication methods means a part-timer can achieve a great deal in limited hours. Even more "out there" is that most staff pay their own fares, and flying from New Zealand to anywhere is not cheap. We sit on the edge of the world, thousands of miles from partners.

Isn't this extremely limiting, you ask? To the contrary, it produces amazing, totally dedicated, missions-loving individuals who love Christ and their partners with great passion. Their treasure is in heaven. They see the sacrifice as a joy, not a burden. The effect on the partners they work with is electrifying. It lifts the bar of performance like little else.

Does it work? My goodness, it does. BHW has a committed team of high-calibre people who manage a wide range of issues with great skill and wisdom. There are lawyers, farmers, accountants, policemen, management consultants, property developers and semi-retired business people, among others. They say their accountability is to the Lord, not a pay packet. It is a useful tool on the mission field too. Encouraging leaders to multi-task ensures a wise use of resources. Many are already doing it out of survival, but where it can be encouraged, it is a sensible way to widen a ministry.

Current NGO Mode

Too often, churches involved in missions and NGOs are caught in a trap. Their dilemmas usually include:

1. High overheads and crippling administration costs. Despite efforts to rein in expenditures and the pressure of exposure, many groups are unable to change the ratio of field outputs to overheads. In the worst instances, over 50% of income goes toward administration. Some others manage to hide overhead costs in the field account. Donors want accountability, honesty, and a low-cost, business-like performance.

2. Too many field efforts are maintaining a dependency culture. Often the motives are good but the execution is poor. We have seen too many instances of damage done by aid that creates a "cargo cult" mentality and ongoing dependency. Shape your missions policy around resourcing the local people to feed and care for themselves. They can do it.

3. Paying international wages. Controversial I guess, but it is just so sad and frustrating to see highly resourced charities and Christian missions with flashy vehicles, handing out unnecessary items, with top paid executives and staff doing six or seven hours a day before retiring back to the best hotel in the nearest town. The locals notice. They wonder whether the work is for them and their needs, or the mission team wages.

You may be wondering, "How on earth are we going to get staff and people to go on missions if they are not well covered with a good income and good facilities?" The truth is, I simply do not know, but I do know One who will supply all my needs in Christ Jesus. There may be a lot more people out there willing to make sacrifices than you expect, and if there are not, then maybe the message is wrong.

BHW people stay with their partners where it is at all possible. The partners love and respect the sacrifice being made and fully understand that their project is getting the funding and not some hotel back in the city. Of course, it has its moments. I (Owen) have laid down to sleep on a clean clay floor in a hut with a thatched roof in Nepal, and wondered in the half light of the stars what the dark, sinister-looking animals were running up and down the pole just above my head. I have a highlighted, very advanced case of incurable murophobia, so on being told they had a problem with rats nesting in the thatch, I was outside sleeping with the cows and pigs. God shut down my brain (not a big ask) and I was soundly asleep in minutes.

Managing relationships is important for BHW to retain integrity and avoid misunderstanding. Every attempt is made to handle all communication between the donor and the field through BHW staff. History shows that allowing direct access leads to difficulties with the partner becoming confused as to where their allegiances lie. Donors generally do not have the detailed understanding of the partner's situation and in some instances are seeking quick fix solutions. While BHW encourages donors to better understand the partner's position and will take to the field on occasional visits, experience shows there is no value in direct communication and often harm is done.

It is worth noting that when money is given by an individual, a church, a trust, or the like, it is given to the Lord. The biblical principle is that we are responding to the bounty of the Lord and worshipping Him with what we have been given. Jesus said,

"When you give ... your Father who sees what is done in secret will reward you" (Matthew 6:3-4). When we give, we are not simply adding to the church budget, we are giving up a thank offering to the Father Himself. To then demand that "my money" be used for a specific purpose is counter to what the Lord seeks. It is a trap that sadly, many fall into. None of us - small givers or large donors - should give money because we feel we have to, or because it makes us feel good. Our starting point should be that it is all God's resources and we are using some for ourselves and the rest is a love offering in response to the riches of grace we receive in Christ.

Partner Example 2: Emmanuel – Knowing God's Business

I (Owen) stepped out into the foyer of the YMCA in Chennai before 7:00a.m. ready to meet the local BHW partners when I heard my name called. Emmanuel Kumar stepped forward. He had travelled all afternoon and through the night in a train sitting on a wooden seat so he could meet me. He was primed and ready to go. "Will you help me, please? I have two burdens on my heart. There are lepers in my town who are not being cared for properly. They have very little food and no medical help, and the children cannot get schooling. Also, there are women in our state who are abused, have nothing, and their lives and their children's lives are ruined. I have plans to help them, but I need some help to get started."

Emmanuel seemed like a genuine leader, but often looks can be deceptive. Some people posing as pastors are frauds deceiving their own people, as well as mission organizations. So BHW began a process of due diligence, seeking information about Emmanuel. It does not take long to ascertain sincerity or otherwise, but BHW takes their time checking and building a relationship with the potential partner.

The leper feeding and caring program ensures some 300 outcasts get at least three good meals per week (they have access to some other food - scraps, leftovers, etc.) and their numerous wounds get attention. Their children are no longer kept in the compound and now gain schooling and a more normal life.

Emmanuel's plans for the destitute women of his town involved setting up training courses to teach sewing. After a year-long course, those who graduate receive a foot-operated treadle sewing machine. At the training course, the women are introduced to Jesus Christ and the Bible and within the year most have come to faith in Christ.

The women gain the ability to make their own clothes and those for their family, as well as selling others in the market. The little independence does wonders for them. The cost for a woman to do the course and receive a sewing machine is less than $100 per year. Multiple courses across the region have been completed.

Anaya had no idea who Jesus Christ was or what a Bible said. Her sister invited her to go with her to sewing classes run by Christians in her village. She was frightened by the idea because she knew that some local Hindu leaders were opposed to any Christian presence in their area. What she experienced amazed her. She had never encountered such a happy group of women, and their singing was bright and joyful. Anaya quickly saw the benefits of learning to sew. She envisaged being able to make her children new outfits and maybe even sell some to help their parlous finances.

Later that night, her husband tried to find out where she had been. Anaya was very reluctant to tell him - she knew it may have disastrous consequences. After attending several sewing classes,

Anaya came home one evening to find a rowdy group of men waiting for her. They grabbed her and pinned her against the wall, demanding to know where she had been. Too frightened to do anything other than explain the truth, she found herself hurled onto the ground. The men lifted up rocks, ready to stone her. They held off but made it clear if she went back they would stone her. She knew her husband was involved.

After missing some classes, Anaya decided she simply wanted to hear more about the Savior who loved her and had died for her sins. She decided to risk it. She had sat down with her husband and explained what she had heard, impressing on him what a wonderful person she had met, called Jesus Christ. She wanted her husband to learn something of her discovery. Her husband was so taken with how happy, contented, cooperative and supportive she was, that he decided to protect her and cut himself off from the Hindu radicals. He wanted to know what she had got involved in. Such is the power of the gospel.

To help ensure accountability and maintain low overheads, BHW gave Emmanuel a small, low-cost camera that records the date on each photo. He covers his activities once a month so BHW knows what is happening. BHW could not have done this project assessment itself. The locals know best, and mostly all they need is the resources to get their project going. Over 1,000 women have been through the course in the Godavari region, most have come to trust Jesus as their Savior, and many have led family members to the Lord.

It is a project that reaches the poorest of the poor and meets both spiritual and temporal needs. It is highly cost-effective and ensures that the women saved are baptized and become part of a local church. Discipling is working well but managed by the partner.

Partner Example 3: T. Raja

Truths

T. Raja owned a tuk tuk and worked as a taxi driver in Bangalore. T. Raja was a Hindu. He knew the vicious, dehumanizing caste system and what it was like to be ostracized. Whole sectors of the Indian community are considered "untouchable." They are the Dalit caste—the lowest order in the five main groupings. They are discarded by the higher castes.

One day, T. Raja heard the story of the Good Samaritan from the Christians' Bible. It

A major aspect of missions is sharing God's grace and love for those in great need. A unique hallmark of Christianity, as opposed to most other world faiths, is compassion for the lost and the totally bereft. Sacrifice and active, practical love that is non-judgemental and seeks only the best in others without seeking anything in return is what Christ ably demonstrated and seeks from us.

fascinated him because he understood the strength of feeling between different groups in society. The story kept going around and around in his head. He and his wife became Christians. His life and outlook changed.

As he scuttled along the street in his tuk tuk with his passengers, dodging and weaving the crazy traffic and cows he saw, the growing numbers of beggars and outcasts dying in the gutter, something suddenly struck him like a bolt from the blue. He could do what the Samaritan man did. It was a Holy Spirit moment. As only the Spirit of God can do with the so few words of Scripture, T. Raja was arrested by the simple but profound grace of Jesus. He had the means to carry them to a little room at his house. He could be a Good Samaritan.

Dropping his bewildered passengers he quickly returned to where he had seen a corpse-like figure cowering on the footpath, emaciated, covered in head lice, only partially clothed, with maggots already infesting a leg wound. Somehow, to T. Raja's own great surprise, he found the strength and grace to pick up the dying beggar and place him in his tuk tuk, gently carrying him home. Those who saw were amazed. No one ever touched a Dalit. You crossed the road to the other side, rather than be near one.

T. Raja had no idea what his wife would think, and no idea what he would do with the beggar, how he would feed him or deal with his life-threatening condition. He had no medical experience and was normally put off by beggars, wounds, maggots, blood, and the like. Somehow, though, it worked out. Room was found, food was shared, and T. Raja found the fortitude to clean the infested wounds, bathe the man, and clothe him in something respectable.

The next day, there was another person in need, abandoned by family and society. And then another. A visit to the rubbish dump led to an extraordinary discovery. In the filth and smelly rubbish, a couple of mangy dogs were playing with what looked like a rag doll. As T. Raja watched, he thought the "doll" moved. He rushed over while others turned away. It was a baby girl, barely alive. The dogs had already eaten her cheek and one eye, part of an arm, and a leg. T. Raja picked her up, took her home, and stitched up her wounds. He cared for her and she became part of a growing family.

People noticed. Some shopkeepers gave him dated food instead of throwing it out. Medical clinics gave him old bandages. A ministry was born - a ministry of compassion and healing. A powerful example to a graceless society. The Holy Spirit brought T. Raja and BHW together. The first reaction was to try to change much of what T. Raja was doing and to steer his plans in a more practical direction. BHW held back from such advice. They simply resourced him to carry on.

The measure of T. Raja's faith and commitment was that he and his wife and children chose to live in a small basement in his house so the entire main part of the house could be used for those he rescued and sought to restore. When his house became too small, he moved to much larger premises. To date,

A Challenge for You

Christians can help combat this evil, degrading business. At the "bottom of the cliff," you can help various agencies that work on the streets rescuing trapped girls.

At the "top of the cliff" are many groups working to provide girls with meaningful work, help lift incomes generally (especially among the hill tribes of Southeast Asia), change social mores that treat girls and women so badly, and stop the trading of not just young girls, but the growing number of young boys demanded by the grossly sordid, de-humanizing, evil business.

T. Raja and his wife, Devi, have picked up 5,000 homeless, sick and injured persons and ministered to their needs.

This is a great story because of the compassion and energy of one man, his vision and faith, and the impact he has made on thousands of lives. It didn't need a missionary to go to India to make this happen. It didn't need a church to raise the $50,000 to $70,000 a year to support a family to leave their home and set up in a foreign land, with a foreign language and foreign customs to learn. The Christian worker with an effective plan and the heart of love was already there. All he needed was some resources.

Scene – Injustice Abounds

Pastor Ng was feeling very positive. He had saved enough petrol to be able to visit some new villages in the hills around Chiang Mai in Thailand. He knew several places where there was little or no Christian witness, and at last he had the opportunity to visit them. He had plans to have the children join the Good News Team ministry in Bangkok; he had some basic handouts and a couple of Thai language Bibles. He was happy.

As he bumped along the gravel road in the stifling heat, he stopped at a place to get something to drink. There he met a person dressed in European clothes and definitely not a local. He greeted him and asked him what he was doing so far from any town, because he was intrigued.

Without missing a beat, the young man told him he was going to the next village to buy girls for some Bangkok bars who needed young, attractive dancers. Ng was shattered. He knew exactly what this meant. They might appear to be just dancers, but in fact, the girls were needed for the sex trade and the demand was for very young girls - even as young as five and six year olds. The young man showed Ng a purse packed full of high denomination baht - clearly enough to buy many girls. In the yard was an old truck with cattle sides. Ng knew what that was for.

A plan formed in Ng's mind. He knew the villagers would be wooed by the money and the embellished story of their daughters becoming well-known dancers in Bangkok. Parents of pretty girls could earn two to three years worth of income in a sale, and also have the girl send home earnings from their work. Ng would have to work fast if he was going to stop the tragedy from occurring. He changed plans and raced back to Chiang Mai. Within 24 hours, he achieved a small miracle - he raised a large sum of money, mostly from concerned, non-Christian businessmen, and left for the village. He arrived the next day planning to offer the villagers financial aid for a number of projects he knew would be helpful. To his great dismay, he was too late. There was not a girl over the age of eight years old left in the village. He was shattered. As he looked into the eyes of the villagers, he knew that they knew. Girls are not highly regarded among the poor in Thailand, and the thought of so much cash lured them away. The girls would join the estimated 400,000 underage girls forced into prostitution in Southeast Asia.

La Mai Coffee

One of the things we like about BHW is that it is unashamedly into commercial solutions. Among the many things it does is sell a very high quality Thai coffee called La Mai. In the rolling hills along the Thai border with Myanmar are multiple tribes of people, many of whom made their living from growing opium poppies. Despite the huge street value, the locals made little out of growing the drug - it was the middlemen who made the millions. BHW sought out a suitable partner in Thailand to help them take some concrete action to help the hill tribe people find alternatives to opium. That partner became the Integrated Tribal Development Program (ITDP) run by Mike Mann and his wife Becky. Mike is a big-hearted American, and Becky a local. They had done work with coffee beans before, so BHW suggested they plant and harvest, and BHW would do the marketing. They put up some funding to make it all happen.

A great partnership has been formed. The coffee has been amazingly successful and the ITDP has done a simply incredible job of finding the best varieties, teaching the hill people how to grow it, setting up harvesting techniques and processes, and making a high value crop available for BHW to market. Today, BHW markets the product in New Zealand and Australia. Over many years, the same hill tribe people have willingly sold their daughters into the sex trade in Bangkok. Girls have not been wanted, as they were deemed to be low value for work. Not only that, she would earn big money accommodating up to a dozen Westerners a night for some club or bar where the bar owner took the lion's share and the daughter would send most of the rest home.

It is hard for us to understand how this can happen. What sort of parents sell their daughters into prostitution, particularly at such a young age? It seems so degrading and unthinkable. Girls are herded up like cattle and carted down to Bangkok in trucks, then hosed down to keep them cool and clean them up. Many are forced into drugs to hook them into staying, and escaping can lead to never being seen again. It is a tragic sight to see these young girls, their eyes dull and lifeless, being sold in bars like pieces of meat. Prostitution is supposed to be illegal in Thailand, but it is known that even politicians and influential businessmen have a stake in this horrendous, sleazy activity. Tragically, it is part of a long-established culture where human life is not held in esteem.

BHW decided that the coffee profits would go into supporting people who worked to rescue girls from the sex trade - a dangerous and difficult work, given the police are usually bribed by the bar owners. There are a number of organizations, both Christian and humanitarian, who work the streets to help girls escape.

The other part of the profits goes to Christian organizations that work to change the culture, to bring the message of love and hope in Christ, to train parents and families to revere life and avoid the plague of sex trafficking. One such ministry works through children, reaching them at a young age with Bible lessons, school visits, and several different means. Thousands of families have been reached and have experienced the love of Jesus. Now these children are grown up and are starting churches throughout Thailand. God is doing amazing things in that country, breaking down the former strongholds of Satan.

The coffee growing is also changing lives. Through ITDP, Mike and Becky have done a simply incredible job among the hill tribes. Not only has the coffee growing been a commercial success, but many of these village people have become Christians. BHW often gets asked whether the coffee project has any beneficial effect among the hill tribe people at a spiritual level. During a recent visit to the growers, we had a village meeting. I asked the village leaders how many people were Christians. Back came the answer through the interpreter: "All." I thought I had been misunderstood. I asked again, trying to clarify, but back came the answer, "We do not know of any person in the village who has not made a personal decision to follow Christ as their Savior and Lord." Wow! Doesn't that thrill you?

You could be involved in a mission like this just by buying the right brand of coffee. Buying La Mai coffee is a way of discipling. Yes, it is different and indirect, but it demonstrates that there are multiple ways to obey the call of Jesus.

REPRESENT
CHAPTER REFLECTIONS

INDIVIDUALS

PRAY

1. Spend time on your knees seeking how you can be involved in global missions in an effective way.

2. Ask the Lord to increase your compassion for the lost and the needy.

3. Seek ways to better understand the needs of a global missions organization.

ENGAGE

1. How can you improve your giving to advance the gospel internationally?

2. Discuss with your home group how to combat paternalism and the lack of respect that occurs in some global missions.

3. Think of ways that you can better support and encourage those on the field.

GO

1. Contact a global missions group that is carrying out Christ's command diligently and effectively, and ask how you can assist them.

2. Contact the La Mai coffee group and ask how you can help.

Churches

Pray

1. Spend time on your knees seeking how to be more effective as a church in global missions.

2. Ask the Lord for guidance in building a more strategic approach to missions.

3. Seek direction from the Lord regarding who your church could partner with in global missions.

Engage

1. Create a missions plan based on what you have learned from the Bright Hope World example.

2. Locate organizations like Bright Hope World who use commercial activities (example: La Mai coffee) to fund and further global missions, and work with them.

3. How can your church ensure that you have genuine partnerships between those in the field and those in the church, and vice versa?

Go

1. Have your pastor and top team visit a developing country with a missions organization so they can see the problems and challenges firsthand.

2. Start a missions team devoted to daily prayer for a missions organization and work with them so you can pray in a detailed, knowing way.

Chapter 9

Recap

Where to from here?
Some conclusions and next steps.

"Kid, you'll move mountains! Today is your day!
Your mountain is waiting. So get on your way!"

– Dr. Seuss

"Go back?" he thought. "No good at all! Go sideways? Impossible!
Go forward? Only thing to do! On we go!"

– J.R.R. Tolkien, The Hobbit

God's purpose in Christ is to reconcile all things to Himself to the praise of His glory. The church is the body of Christ in the world - the means by which the world will know that Jesus Christ is Lord, and through which all believers will reach maturity in Christ and unity in the faith and knowledge of Christ.

To fulfill His mission to reconcile all things to Himself God sends you and me, into the world to spread the gospel, to evangelize, to proclaim the good news of the Kingdom of God, to make disciples and to take up the challenge of being reconcilors. Lofty words indeed. God is God. He will achieve His ends. We can either be part of His plans or we can hide in the shadows. Jesus did not shrink back from giving us instructions. He was blunt, direct and authoritative. No room for discussion, shades of meaning, different interpretations. As they say, "Which part of 'go' don't you understand?" Just "go." Not a call, but a command. The "go" may be a walk across the street to help and witness to a neighbor, it may be picking up the phone and calling someone hurting, sitting down with a sports team member, or going to Uganda. It's the obedience mindset that counts. It is the passion in your heart that counts.

We either obey or we deliberately choose to disobey. What becomes apparent is that the "go" involves all manner of activities that generally lead to new converts and them being baptized and discipled. Some will give, some will pray, some will travel, some will write letters, some will encourage, some will write books, some will preach, evangelize, teach, support and more.

That diversity, coupled with our limited resources, demands a plan, some coherence to how we achieve this command of Jesus. It is about being strategic. It is a role we play as an individual, but it is also carried out at churches where our inputs can be multiplied, organized in a plan and enhanced.

What Does a Missions' Plan Look Like?

1. It starts on our knees. Men and women, husbands, wives, dads, moms, families committed to praying and seeking God for what role they play in the Great Commission. For churches, it starts at the top. Pastors and elders fully committed to praying and seeking God for how they will lead and moblize their disciples to live on mission daily.

2. It must be a biblically-based vision and a written down strategy. It must involve everyone in the church where each person is assigned a task that matches their passions, their personal call and their ability with what the strategy needs.

3. It must be led from the top. The lead pastor and the elders set the pace and tone in the church. An effective missions plan needs not just a tacit blessing from the top, but active, visible ownership and management.

4. It should involve inputs in all areas of witnessing, evangelising and discipling from the home through the local area, nationally and globally. Training in and practicing witnessing should be regular events.

5. The plan needs to foster interest, passion for the lost, training for missions and witnessing, gain a significant share of the budget, stimulate regular church, small group, and individual mention and discussion on missions.

6. Be resourceful and inventive. Apply the same or more energy to missions as you do to the worship time. Since two-thirds of the "unreached" live in countries that are not accessible to American missionaries, the best strategy is to find the national Christians that God is using in places where we can't go. Invest in special projects that can multiply the effectiveness of their work, such as Christian satellite TV broadcasts, Internet evangelism and discipleship, social media, Bibles, training materials and micro-business investments that will lead to self-sustainability.

7. Focus on partnership. Respect, resource and nurture those who already have a plan, know their circumstances better than you and only need your help to fly. Aim for cost-effectiveness, accountability, sustainability and fostering independence among the poorest of the poor.

8. Aim to deliver the complete package. Missions involves evangelism, baptizing, discipling, church planting and a focus on the poor, the defenseless and those suffering from injustice.

9. Remember the 25:1 rule. You can have 25 local missionaries for less than it costs to send one of your own. They will normally work from Day One, understand the local scene better, have fewer cultural issues and reach more people. They are out there waiting for you to resource and encourage them.

10. Focus on enthusing your young people regarding missions. They are the future. Invest heavily in ensuring they are sorted doctrinally, then set them alight in missions.

The essence of missions can be summed up in the following diagram:

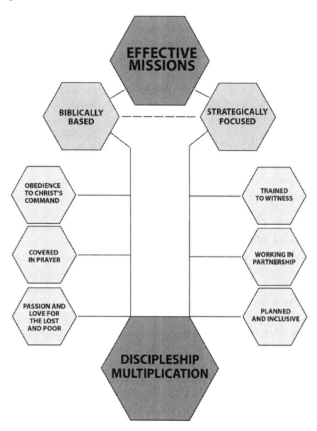

Here is a checklist of principles and practices that you and your church could run through every few months as a means of assessing your effectiveness in missions:

Prayer

Prayer is the fuel of all outreach and missions. We must be regularly and deliberately on our knees seeking His will. It is not about asking God to bless our efforts, but us getting on board with His vision for us. Prayer is the privilege we have to unite our hearts to God and His plans. Assess the intensity of your own prayer time and that of your church.

Bible

God's Word reveals the Father's heart for the nations. From the beginning to the end, the Bible is a story of God's love for mankind and His reaching out. As we learn the story of this God and His plan of redemption for mankind this will impel us forward to share the Good News of Jesus to those with whom we interact daily.

Holy Spirit

Jesus told the apostles to wait in Jerusalem for the Holy Spirit to come before they went out to make disciples and fulfill the task of reaching the nations with the gospel. We need the power of the Holy Spirit to lead us, guide us, empower us and help us for the great task that Jesus has left for us. We don't need more of the Holy Spirit, as some seek; He needs more of us. There are no shortcuts or easy pathways to God's blessing.

Worship

The goal of missions is for every tribe, nation, people and language to worship the King of Kings and the Lord of Lords, Jesus Christ. We should find ways for the worship that is done in our churches to pour into our homes, communities, nations and world. Everything that we do is for God's glory through the everydayness of life.

Disciple

Jesus was clear: We are to follow Him and die to ourselves daily by taking up our cross. We live for God's glory and His purpose. We allow Christ's agenda to be our agenda to advance His Kingdom here on earth. We are called to something deeper than just pursuing what the world has to offer. Seek to be a disciple and disciple others. Rate your progress.

Multiplication

Jesus is not interested in us making converts. He does the saving. We are to make fully devoted disciples through baptism, helping people die to themselves and be united into Jesus' death, burial, and resurrection, and teaching them the commands of God. It is not about just getting people to pray a prayer and be done. It is a long-term investment to help believers move from belief to obedience. Be dedicated to making disciples who will make other disciples. Can you name someone you've impacted through discipling in the last month?

Sending

We are called to be sent. Jesus was sent and He is sending us as His witnesses, and we are to be so with full joy. Churches are to be sending agencies of mobilized, trained and equipped passionate disciple-makers to reach the nations. We are commanded to go to all nations and teach them everything Christ has taught us. How many have been sent from your church this last year?

Unreached

It is a tragedy that still today, more than six thousand people groups and over two billion individuals have yet to hear the name of Jesus and come to a saving faith in Him. Very little funding and very few missionaries are heading to the areas where the unreached live. We need to seek innovative ways that we can partner with Jesus to advance His renown. Look for bi-vocational opportunities. We must not settle for anything less. To gain a better understanding of unreached people, visit the Joshua Project online at https://joshuaproject.net.

Caring

Supporting a missionary is more than sending a check once in a while. It is about daily praying for them and blessing them generously. This can be achieved through a variety of means and doesn't necessarily have to cost you much in time and giving. Your care can be through regular encouragement, remembering personal significant dates throughout the year, sending packages to brighten their days, etc. Your support, encouragement and love can help ensure healthy individuals and marriages for those on the field. Review your own and your church's efforts over the last month in this area.

Learning

Never stop studying and understanding people and the culture around you. Become a lifelong learner of His Word. Read books, discover missionary biographies, talk to missionaries, collaborate with other churches to see what others are doing, keep up-to-date with news from the field and allow this to be communicated to others for effective and efficient care and prayers.

Vision and Strategy

A clear and compelling vision gives direction, meaning and purpose. It allows people to understand what it is you are seeking to do. It is a basis for growing enthusiasm. Let God be the cornerstone, and ask the Holy Spirit to lead and guide you as you seek to develop a global outreach ministry. Understand the DNA and culture of your church, then match the passions and talents available for effective discipleship and global evangelism. Look to see how you can maximize the resources you have for Kingdom growth. Global outreach should just be an extension of your church's local ministry. When did you last revisit your church's strategy on global outreach?

Focus

There are many social injustices globally. It is easy to get overwhelmed and try to take on too much. Take small steps to work in areas that tug at your heart, and do them well. Narrow the focus to be more effective with the resources you are entrusted with.

Partnership

Maximize your effectiveness by working in tight partnerships where respect and dignity reign. Seek opportunities to work together; the task is too great for one disciple, church, denomination, or organization to see the gospel taken to all nations. There is power in numbers when we all work together.

Focus on what we have in common, not what separates us. Make unity work amongst Christians in your area.

Humility and Servanthood

Disciples should be known by their love through serving and meeting the needs of others. It is about giving and providing for others beyond what they may expect or demand. It is not for our benefit, but for God to be glorified. How many feet have you washed lately besides your own?

Passionfruit – Compassion and Passion Bearing Fruit

Oh, for more passion and compassion. When you have the privilege of serving others, do so with vitality and fervency. Add gentleness, humility and respect. Seek to understand others needs, where they are at, what will really help, and how you can help them get to where they want to be. Treat every person with dignity and compassion as an individual, not some project or task to be completed or worked on. Review your own progress on producing the fruit of the Spirit in your life.

Sustainability

It is important to understand that poverty is more than just a state of being poor. There are many differing circumstances that lead to people becoming poor. The task is to help the underprivileged deal with the injustices and circumstances that have led them to the position they are in, and to move them into a better state of mind and wellbeing. You must help them focus on their available resources and empower them to take ownership of their situation, grow in independence, and not rely solely on outside support to move them to a better position.

Stewardship

Be a wise and faithful steward of the resources available. Don't lose sight of the fact that much can be achieved with a little. We have a generous God.

Hey, that's it. We are all done.

Discipleship is all a matter of faith and obedience that is biblically based and strategically focused. We hope and pray that God has stirred something deep inside of you to live more passionately and purposefully. Every day we have is a gift, and we can use these gifts to bless others with the hope of the Good News of Jesus Christ. Take up the challenge to put your life right with God and yield yourself wholly to Him. Be an instrument He can use. Then help your church to be a missions' focused church committed to the urgent need of lost souls wherever they are.

You can do it. You are in the best team with the best resources. Go for it. Our lives should be used by God and for His eternal glory.

Recap
Chapter Reflections

Individuals

Pray

1. Allow the Holy Spirit to lead you on your next steps in missions.

2. Spend time on your knees praying about how your life can be used by God and for His glory.

3. Pray for God to develop a deeper sense of obedience in your heart.

Engage

1. Keep a diary and a checklist of things that you may be able to do, then review your progress from time to time. Pray about how to increase your effectiveness.

2. Find ways to raise the subject of missions, witnessing, missionaries, partnering, etc. whenever you are meeting with other people from your church. Slip it into the conversation.

3. Have your children learn more about missionaries and partnerships. Make pen pals with missionary kids and study developing countries on the map and on the internet.

Go

1. Plan on going on a trip to visit a missionary to understand life in their shoes for a short period of time.

2. Seek out ways that your family can intentionally serve others locally, nationally, or globally. Make a plan to do this within the next six to twelve months.

Churches

Pray

1. Spend time on your knees praying for church members to have a heart for evangelism and for equipping the church for reaching the lost.

2. Pray for the right strategy for your church to engage effectively in global missions.

3. Intercede for your leadership and pastors as they lead your church.

Engage

1. How can your church make missions more central to the church's activities and budget?

2. Make sure your children's and student ministries have missions content taught regularly. Help cultivate an understanding of global missions and develop a love for the nations early in life.

3. Develop strategies in your church regarding how you can regularly be praying, caring for and supporting those serving cross-culturally.

Go

1. Plan to visit your mission partners or plan to visit new fields.

2. Plan for your church to be a sending church of young and old alike to the field for the short and long term.

Appendix One

Helps

Helpful Organizations:

This is not an exhaustive list of mission organizations. There are many hundreds of groups working tirelessly on the Great Commission. However, if you are interested, these groups offer excellent starting places.

MiT – Missionaries in Training
Based in Springfield, Ohio
www.mitglobal.org

Missionaries in Training, a wok begin and managed by Andrew, is a strategy of global missions multiplication through intentional, relational, and deliberate discipleship for fueling young people's passions for a global purpose. Here individuals or churches can find information on taking their next step.

Bright Hope World
Based in Christchurch, New Zealand
www.brighthopeworld.com

Bright Hope World is focused on partnerships in developing countries among the poorest of the poor. Holistic approach to development, rehabilitation and advocacy as well as evangelism and discipling.

Team Expansion
Based in Louisville, Kentucky, USA
www.teamexpansion.org

Committed to reaching the unreached. Their desire is to see every person in the world reached with the gospel of Christ. They are working toward that goal through evangelism, church planting, and disciple making movements. A sending organization focused on church planting, evangelism, and baptism, with over 350 full-time workers.

TRAIN International
Based in Joplin, Missouri, USA
www.traininternational.org

TRAIN International equips individuals and teams preparing to live and work cross-culturally, and provides debriefing when they return from the field. TRAIN International also offers coaching to churches who are sending and supporting cross-cultural workers. Their goal is that workers go prepared, stay effective, and return healthy and prepared for their next phase of ministry.

Good News Productions International
Based in Joplin, Missouri, USA
gnpi.org

GNPI equips the body of Christ with culturally relevant media and technology to accelerate global evangelism.

ICOM
Based in Clayton, Indiana, USA
theicom.org

The International Conference on Missions (ICOM) exists to encourage, equip, and enlist workers for the harvest. This is a conference held by members of the Christian Church/Church of Christ. Each year the conference is in differing cities around the U.S.

Christian Missionary Fellowship International
Based in Indianapolis, Indiana, USA
www.cmfi.org

Christian Missionary Fellowship creates dynamic Christ-centered communities that transform the world. Currently serving in 25 countries, its areas of emphasis include planting churches, serving the urban poor, reaching out to university students, and opening doors in resistant countries.

Joshua Project
Based in Colorado Springs, Colorado, USA
joshuaproject.net

Joshua Project is a research initiative seeking to highlight the ethnic people groups of the world with the fewest followers of Christ. Accurate, updated, ethnic people group information is critical for understanding and completing the Great Commission. Revelation 5:9 and 7:9-10 show that there will be some from every tribe, tongue, nation, and people before the throne.

Appendix Two

For the Stats Fans

Some people are fascinated by statistics. They can tell startling stories. The stories can also be dismissed without having the intended effect. Sometimes discussion about the millions around the world who do not know Christ just misses the mark. We want to give up before we start. The big numbers are daunting. "How can I reach the millions in India?" or "I don't have the ability to make an impression on the huge numbers of unsaved in my town, let alone the world."

It is the same problem as "How do I eat an elephant?" Answer? One mouthful at a time. If a couple of Christians set about committed witnessing, it would be surprising just how short a time it would take to see your whole town come to Christ. It works especially well if you adopt the compounding effect.

Take a hypothetical case. Let's say 100 people in your church get fired up about missions and discipling. Let's say that they each lead two people to Christ each month for a whole year. Let's also say that each one they lead to Christ does the same thing—leads two people each to the Lord. In 12 months, that group of 100 Christians would have brought over 53 million people into the Kingdom. Yeah, yeah, it's not very likely, but it shows two things:

First, we are underperforming badly as a church worldwide. Second, it's not such a daunting task after all to see the world changed for Christ.

The Muslim community has a different way of achieving their goals, but use similar math. If every Muslim family in Europe has the typical five or six children in their family, they will out vote non-Muslims by 2035 in most European countries. Compounding has an amazing effect.

When Jesus instructed us on prayer, He said, "Give us this day our daily bread." He didn't say "weekly bread" or "monthly bread." Let us move forward one day at a time with the resources of the day.

Disturbing Statistics About the Church in the USA:

- 85% of all funding goes toward internal operations
- 50% to pay the salary of pastors and church staff
- 22% to pay for upkeep and expansion of buildings
- 13% for church expenses such as electricity and supplies
- 15% outreach (includes 3% for local missions)
- 2% for overseas missions (both evangelistic and charitable)

In the end, if you only give to your local church, odds are that only 2% of 2.58% (average giving out of your income in the USA), or 0.05% of your income is going toward "preaching the gospel to every nation" and helping the "poorest of the poor" combined. To put that in perspective, if you make $50,000 a year, that is only $25.80 per year. That is less than the average spent on one visit to a casual dining restaurant in the USA.

Until recently, Americans gave less money to reach the unreached than they spent buying Halloween costumes ... for their pets.

There are 886,052 international students in the U.S. Only 10% have any contact with an evangelical church. Shockingly, 80% never get to visit an American home.

There are 78,000 Evangelical Christians for every one unreached people group.

Of all Christian workers, 95% are working within the Christian world.

For every $100,000 that Christians make, they give $1 to the unreached.

Evangelical Christians could provide all of the funds needed to plant a church in each of the 6,900 unreached people groups with only 0.03% of their income.

BHW can feed 100 kids for a week on what you spend on a tube of lipstick. It takes so little to make a difference in developing countries.

Ninety percent of foreign missionaries work among already reached people groups. Ten percent work among unreached people groups (Winter and Koch, 543).[25]

There are more churches in the Dallas/Fort Worth area than there are Christian North American missionaries to 1,930,000,000 Muslim, Hindu, Han Chinese and Buddhist people who have not been reached by the gospel.

Six hundred and fifty Protestant North American missionaries minister to 1.93 million unreached people, while 1 million Christian workers in America minister to 200 million people, most of whom are already reached.

Despite Christ's command to evangelize, approximately 67% of all humans from A.D. 30 to the present day have never even heard the name of Jesus Christ (Baxter 2007, 12).[26]

Christians spend more on the annual audits of their churches and agencies ($810 million) than on all their workers in the non-Christian world (World Evangelization Research Center).[27]

The average American Christian gives only one penny a day to global missions (Yohannan, *Revolution in World Missions*, 142).[28]

Christian organizations spend $8 billion a year on conferences. (Yohannan, *Come Let's Reach the World*, 126).[29]

About the Authors

Andrew Jit was born and raised in New Zealand and has served in various ministry roles in New Zealand and the United States. His passion is helping disciples live on mission daily to have a global impact. He loves to challenge disciples and inspire the next generation to live passionately and radically for God. He has travelled extensively around the world teaching, leading and training disciples. He is married to his beautiful bride, Jamie, and blessed with two daughters, Hannah and Ella.

Owen Jennings is a Christian businessman from New Zealand. He has spent over 30 years involved in local and global missions. Owen has set up partnerships in several third world countries when he worked with Bright Hope World. He and his wife, Doreen, managed a large Christian camp for five years. He has been a successful dairy and beef farmer and was elected the National President of the New Zealand farmers' organisation. He also served for six years as Member of the New Zealand Parliament. Owen and Doreen have four adult children, and ten grandchildren.

SOURCES

---

[1] Hallowell, Bill. (Oct. 30, 2013). *5 Possible Reasons Young Americans Are Leaving Church and Christianity Behind.* Retrieved from http://www.theblaze.com/stories/2013/10/30/5-possible-reasons-young-americans-are-leaving-church-and-christianity-behind/.
Research Releases in Culture & Media (March 24, 2014). *Americans Divided on the Importance of Church.* Retrieved from https://www.barna.org/barna-update/culture/661-americans-divided-on-the-importance-of-church#.VyzWEaMrK1t.

[2] Aldrich, Joe (2006) *Lifestyle Evangelism: Learning to Open Your Life to Those Around You Paperback.* Colorado Springs, CO: Multnomah Books.

[3] Greenfield, Craig (March 4, 2015). Stop calling it a "Short Term Missions Trip". Here's what you should call it instead. [Web log post]. Retrieved December 20, 2015 from http://www.craiggreenfield.com/blog/2015/3/4/stop-calling-it-short-term-missions

[4] *John Stott quotes from Webber, Robert E, (2003) Ancient-Future Evangelism: Making Your Church a Faith-Forming Community. Grand Rapids, MI: Baker Books*

[5] *adapted from* The Star Thrower, *by Loren Eiseley (1907 – 1977)*

[6] Gordon D. Fee, Revelation, New Covenant Commentary Series (Eugene, OR: Cascade Books, 2011)

[7] Ellin, Abby, *The Beat (Up) Generation*, Psychology Today, published on March 11, 2014.
https://www.psychologytoday.com/articles/201403/the-beat-generation

[8] McDowell, Josh *"The Me-ism Culture: Self Is First,"* Josh McDowell's Official Blog, Monday, November 10, 2008 http://joshmcdowell.blogspot.com/2008_11_01_archive.html

[9] McDowell, Josh *"The Me-ism Culture: Self Is First,"* Josh McDowell's Official Blog, Monday, November 10, 2008 http://joshmcdowell.blogspot.com/2008_11_01_archive.html

[10] I McDowell, Josh *"The Me-ism Culture: Self Is First,"* Josh McDowell's Official Blog, Monday, November 10, 2008 http://joshmcdowell.blogspot.com/2008_11_01_archive.html

[11] McDowell, Josh *"The Me-ism Culture: Self Is First,"* Josh McDowell's Official Blog, Monday, November 10, 2008 http://joshmcdowell.blogspot.com/2008_11_01_archive.html

[12] William Wilberforce UK House of Parliament speech 12th May 1789.

[13] *esa.un.org/unpd/wpp/publications/files/key_findings_wpp_2015.pdf*

[14] United Nations Report 2015 ESA/P/WP.241. United Nations, Department of Economic and Social Affairs, Population Division (2015). *World Population Prospects: The 2015 Revision.* New York: United Nations.

[15] Aldrich, Joe (2006) *Lifestyle Evangelism: Learning to Open Your Life to Those Around You Paperback.* Colorado Springs, CO: Multnomah Books.

[16] Hughes, Barbara, Disciplines of a Godly Women, Crossway Publisher, 2001

[17] Worldometers.info (9 May, 2016) *World Population: Past, Present, and Future.* Retrieved from http://www.worldometers.info/world-population/#table-historical.

[18] Charles Hodge. (n.d.). BrainyQuote.com. Retrieved September 8, 2016, from BrainyQuote.com Web site: http://www.brainyquote.com/quotes/quotes/c/charleshod319925.html

[19] Source: 1982 Lausanne Committee Chicago meeting. What is a people group? Source: https://joshuaproject.net/resources/articles/what_is_a_people_group

[20] Just Disney (2016). *Walt Disney, Biography*. Retrieved from http://www.justdisney.com/walt_disney/biography/long_bio.html

[21] Stott, John R. W. (1994) *The Message of Romans: God's good new for the world*. Downers Grove, IL: Inter-Varsity Press. (53).

[22] Platt, David (2014). Divine Sovereignty: The Fuel of Death-Defying Missions in *The Underestimated Gospel* (pp. 55-87). Nashville, TN: B&H Publishing Group.

[23] Platt, David (2014). Divine Sovereignty: The Fuel of Death-Defying Missions in *The Underestimated Gospel* (pp. 55-87). Nashville, TN: B&H Publishing Group.

[24] Global Frontiers Mission (May 23, 2015). *State of the World / The Task Remaining*. Retrieved from https://www.youtube.com/watch?v=WrHC7hXNoV8.

[25] Winter, Ralph D., and Bruce A. Koch. 2009. Finishing the Task: The Unreached Peoples Challenge. In Perspectives on the World Christian Movement: A Reader, ed. Ralph D. Winter and Steven C. Hawthorne, 531-46. Pasadena, CA: William Carey Library. Source: http://www.aboutmissions.org/statistics.html

[26] Baxter, Mark R. 2007. The Coming Revolution: Because Status Quo Missions Won't Finish the Job. Mustang, OK: Tate Publishing. Source: http://www.aboutmissions.org/statistics.html

[27] World Evangelization Research Center. An AD 2001 Reality Check. http://gem-werc.org/gd/findings.htm. Source: http://www.aboutmissions.org/statistics.html

[28] Yohannan, K.P. 2004. Revolution in World Missions. Carrollton, TX: GFA Books. Source: http://www.aboutmissions.org/statistics.htm

[29] Yohannan, K.P. 2004. Come Let's Reach the World. Carrollton, TX: GFA Books.